D1774705

FAMILY SECRETS

FAMILY SECRETS
SECRET STRATEGIES FOR NEW YORK CITY MULTIFAMILY INVESTING

PETER VON DER AHE

Featuring Contributing Expert Authors
Glen Kunofsky
Mark McGorry
Foreword by **Michael Stoler** of *The Stoler Report*

Right Words Press, Corp.
New York, New York

© 2010 Right Words Press, Corp.

All rights reserved. No part of this book may be reproduced or transmitted in any form or by any means, electronic or mechanical, including photocopying, recording, or by any information storage and retrieval system, without permission in writing from the publisher.

Published by
Right Words Press, Corp.
New York, New York
FAMSECRETSBOOK.COM

Publisher's Cataloging-in-Publication Data
Von Der Ahe, Peter.

    Family secrets : secret strategies for New York City multifamily investing / Peter Von Der Ahe. – New York, N.Y. : Right Words Press, Corp., 2010.

    p. ; cm.

    ISBN13: 978-0-9845454-0-7

    1. Apartment houses—Economic aspects—New York (State)—New York. 2. Real estate investment—New York (State)—New York--Cost effectiveness. I. Title.

HD7287.6.U62N7 V66 2010
333.338—dc22   2010926364

Project coordination by Jenkins Group, Inc.
www.BookPublishing.com

FIRST EDITION

Interior layout by Brooke Camfield

Printed in the United States of America
14 13 12 11 10 • 5 4 3 2 1

*To all the landlords and tenants in all the land,
who make this the most interesting job in the world*

*And to my wife,
without whom it would all be meaningless*

Contents

Foreword		ix
You Don't Have to Be Trump		xi
1	Rent Stabilization and How It Works	1
2	Why NYC Real Estate is Unique	19
3	Breakdown of the Multifamily Market	37
4	Out-of-the-Box	51
5	Debt and Equity	63
6	The Role of the Architect in Real Estate Investing	79
7	Winning the Buying and Selling Game	89
8	Property Management	105
9	Net-Lease Investments By Glen Kunofsky	127
10	Trusts and Estates By Mark McGorry	147
Appendix A	Resources for NYC Real Estate Investors	169
Appendix B	Real Estate Glossary	173
References Cited		181
About the Authors		183
For More Information		185

Foreword

The history of New York City residential and commercial real estate is truly full of *Family Secrets*. In the early twentieth century, the true builders of the city of New York arrived from around the world to find their success. Individuals including Joseph Durst, Samuel Rudin, Samuel B. and David Rose, Jack Resnick, Isaac Muss, and Harry LeFrak were the first members of their families to become involved in real estate. Many of them immigrated from Europe and traveled to Ellis Island with the hope of bringing their families to New York. These founders of New York City real estate had humble beginnings as the owners of predominately residential rental apartment buildings in the boroughs of Manhattan, Brooklyn, and Queens.

Today, the Durst Organization owns and operates some of the largest office buildings in New York City. In the early part of the twentieth century, Joseph Durst arrived in America at the age of 13, with $3 sewn in the lapel of his coat. The LeFrak Organization has owned and operated more than 40,000 residential rental apartment buildings in New York City and New Jersey. In 1901, Russian-born Harry LeFrak came to the United States from Palestine and arrived in New York City with $4 in his pocket.

These stories are rather similar to those of other families that arrived in New York and strove to build their companies from humble roots; today they have organizations with thousands of employees and provide housing and office space for residents and businesses in the biggest city in the country.

All of these families, as well as new real estate owners and operators of residential rental buildings, had one thing in common: their roots in real estate began in residential multifamily buildings.

Peter Von Der Ahe, in his book *Family Secrets*, provides the reader with information on New York City multifamily investing. Nothing is easy in life, especially owning and operating real estate. Yet, Mr. Von Der Ahe's book renders valuable guidance on how to own, operate, and become successful in multifamily real estate. His in-depth discussion of the history of rent stabilization, the multifamily market, debt, and equity provides valuable insight into the biggest real estate market in the world.

Billions of dollars have been made and lost in New York City real estate. With *Family Secrets*, you will have the opportunity to learn how it is done.

Michael Stoler,
May 2010

You Don't Have to Be Trump

As long as you're going to be thinking anyway, think big.

—DONALD TRUMP

As a broker who has logged more than 25,000 hours working in New York City, I have an insider's view on its unique, complex market. The job takes me from the rooftops of multistory elevator buildings, down into the basements and subbasements of 100-plus-year-old walk-ups, into the luxurious units of $3,000-per-square-foot pads on 5th Avenue, and into tenements in the Bronx where multiple fire codes have been broken because the units are so overstuffed with immigrants.

I've interacted and done business with first-generationers who have owned their buildings for 65 years and are practically married to their properties. I've worked with owners of 200-plus-bed transient hotels on the Bowery, rent-stabilized properties in the Bronx, and luxury properties on Manhattan's East Side—and everything in between. Some of this is beautiful, some of this is ugly, and most fiction can't touch it, but it is the reality and the truth of New York City multifamily ownership.

What I've found is that there is no such thing as a cookie-cutter approach in the New York City real estate market, as there is in other urban areas of the

United States. After years of working here—and dealing with everyone from owners of single properties to investors who own 1,000 units—I've gathered and seen enough of it and gained experience to be able to write this book and share with you some insider information that you wouldn't have access to if you weren't out there working in the market every day.

You need to know how the players (owners, property managers, superintendents, and tenants, to name just a few) operate in order to create a successful strategy here. You have to understand the rules behind buying and selling properties, how partners interact, and what to do when things get messy and start to unravel. I interact with owners during the two most critical periods in the investment process—the purchase and the sale—and have a circular view of the business that few others have.

New York is like no other market in the world. It's a melting pot of cultures that hail from the Middle East, South America, Asia, all over Europe, and everywhere in between. Each culture brings with it unique negotiation and business styles that you'll be dealing with every day. The owners of real estate here are some of the most interesting people in the world, but their diversity can make for challenging communications and negotiations.

Real estate in this city is hard work, especially when you encounter city officials, property managers, and tenants (or all three) who want something. However, if you can actually deliver value to those you are in business with (be it tenants, bankers, or whomever) in exchange for a profit, then you'll find the upside in the New York real estate market can be extremely rewarding.

I'm here to help you reach that goal. I know the entire continuum of ownership, from the property search and possession to the day-to-day maintenance and the disposal of real estate. There are subcategories within each of those elements, and in this book I've peeled back the first layer in order to get at those nuances that will help you create a successful real estate investment strategy.

I'm not a professional writer, nor am I a book author. But, in 2009 as the number of transactions in the marketplace was tumbling, it was clear that to be productive, I needed to be doing something in addition to moving buildings. So I wrote this book.

I'm just someone who, on a typical day, in a typical morning, can be found in a suit and doing business in a 100-degree boiler room with a 70-year-old Italian immigrant who is reciting 50 years of stories involving tenants, city dealings, trials, and extremes he's been pushed to and accomplishments associated with the building. That same afternoon, I'll be on the fifty-sixth story of Class A office building while I work to create and implement a purchasing and disposal strategy for a multimillion-dollar opportunity fund.

These scenes repeat daily for me and have forced me to learn everything about the New York City real estate market. In this book, I've tapped into this vault of information to come up with the most useful—and sometimes comical—facts. Hopefully, you'll come away with a newfound knowledge of the inner workings of the New York real estate market and an appreciation for its nuances and uniqueness.

In this book, you'll learn about rent stabilization and how it works, get insights into the current economic/real estate conditions in the city, and find out exactly what makes the city's real estate market unique. You'll read real-life anecdotes about the city's property owners, tenants, and superintendents and find out exactly why New York's supply and demand issues are very different from those in other markets. I'll also give you an insider's look at some of the best out-of-the-box deals available in the city and help you make the best debt and equity decisions.

I'll also give you insights into some of the other opportunities in the market. Whether they are upgrading their properties (and in need of an architect), selling their apartment buildings (and in need of financial planning and wealth preservation assistance), or branching out into other areas of the market (and looking for assistance with triple-net leases), the most successful real estate investors collect a vast amount of contacts and information for future use.

As you work your way through this book, keep in mind the fact that all New York City properties come not only with a nugget of immense opportunity for investors but also with their own problems and challenges. Having watched many landlords spend years figuring out what those issues are with their own properties, I've written this book to educate you on those potential pitfalls and help you capitalize on successes.

1
Rent Stabilization and How It Works

It is clear that what the board does—that is, an across-the-board increase for one- and two-year increases—does not target the areas of stabilized stock that need larger increases.

—MARVIN MARKUS, CHAIRMAN,
NYC RENT GUIDELINES BOARD

You cannot begin to understand the New York City multifamily market unless you know the history of its laws. While it remains the only remaining American city with these abysmal laws, rent regulations were originally established to deal with housing shortages and rent gouging that gripped the country's tight housing markets in the 1900s. The federal government stepped in during World War II when President Franklin D. Roosevelt signed the Emergency Price Control Act into law in 1942 and put into effect an official nationwide rent control policy for residential buildings constructed before February 1947.

The federal rent control ended in 1953 when the Korean War was over but continues to influence landlord-tenant laws in certain cities, including New York. New York State picked up where the federal regulation left off, taking a similar approach by regulating rents, services, and evictions for all rental units.

Just the Facts

Rent-controlled apartments are located in buildings constructed before February 1947 in New York State municipalities that didn't declare an end to the postwar rental housing emergency. For a unit to be under rent control, the tenant must have been residing there continuously since before July 1, 1971.

Rent-stabilized apartments are in buildings with six or more units that were built between February 1, 1947, and December 31, 1973. Tenants in buildings constructed prior to February 1, 1947, but who moved in after June 30, 1971, are also covered by rent stabilization.

In 1950, New York State first assumed responsibility for administering rent regulations through the Temporary State Housing Rent Commission. In 1962, New York City began administering its own program. In 1964, the Division of Housing and Community Renewal (DHCR) was given the responsibility of administering rent regulation in municipalities within New York City.

Key Terms to Know

Division of Housing and Community Renewal (DHCR): The New York State agency has primary responsibility for formulating New York State housing policy and monitoring and enforcing the provisions of the state's residential rent regulation laws.

Rent Guidelines Board (RGB): The NYC Rent Guidelines Board is mandated to establish rent adjustments for the approximately one million dwelling units subject to the Rent Stabilization Law in New York City. The board holds an annual series of public meetings and hearings to consider research from staff and testimony from owners, tenants, advocacy groups, and industry experts.

> **Emergency Tenant Protection Act (ETPA):** In Nassau, Rockland, and Westchester counties, this act states that rent stabilization applies to non-rent-controlled apartments in buildings of six or more units built before January 1, 1974, in localities that have declared an emergency and adopted ETPA.

In 1969, New York City expanded the current rent stabilization laws through the enactment of the Rent Stabilization Law of 1969. This new law placed approximately 400,000 previously exempt apartments under a new system of rent regulation.

> **DID YOU KNOW?**
>
> Rent stabilization also covers buildings that are approved for J-51 (the city tax credit for housing improvements) or 421-a (a partial tax exemption to developers of new construction for a period of 10, 15, or 25 years) credits.

In 1971, the state passed several laws designed to gradually deregulate the rent-controlled and rent-stabilized housing stock. In response to tenant concerns about this deregulation, the state passed the Emergency Tenant Protection Act of 1974 (ETPA), which provided for a stabilization system in Nassau, Rockland, and Westchester counties in municipalities choosing to adopt the regulations. The DHCR was directed to implement ETPA in these counties.

The ETPA also amended the New York City Rent Stabilization Law, thereby re-regulating many decontrolled apartments and placing additional buildings under stabilization for the first time. The move was ludicrous and unfounded, but it stuck. In 1983, the state gave DHCR the responsibility for administering New York City's rent control and rent stabilization programs. This took effect in 1984 and doubled DHCR's size. To put this in perspective, it should be noted that New York City has approximately 960,000 of the one million units that are regulated statewide (http://www.dhcr.state.ny.us/).

I don't know . . . I assume so . . .

The New York Story

In New York City, in units subject to rent stabilization, tenants are shielded from sharp increases in rent and retain the right to renew their leases. The city's Rent Guidelines Board (RGB) determines what percentage of rent increases are allowed each year.

New York reigns as the city with the longest history of rent regulation. Spurred on by a lack of decent housing for the masses, rent stabilization has essentially become a way of life for many city residents. The regulations have been in force for so long that many renters in the system can't wrap their minds around the more "traditional" way of renting apartments.

> **Did You Know?**
>
> Today, approximately one million of New York City's rental housing accommodations are subject to rent regulation.

All of this regulation begs a question: why own property here? For investors, the most recent overhaul of the rent laws took place in 1997, with the passage of the Rent Regulation Reform Act. One of the more landlord-friendly laws to be passed, the New York Housing Law, provided this new formula for computing the rent increases for stabilized apartments that become vacant:

> For vacancy leases: 20 percent if the tenant chooses a two-year lease, 16 percent if the tenant chooses a one-year lease. The vacancy increase for one-year leases is determined each year by taking 20 percent minus the difference between one- and two-year-renewal leases. Under the most recent rent guidelines period, the difference is 4 percent, so 20 percent – 4 percent = 16 percent. (Note: these amounts are subject to change, but this is the general range we have seen.)
>
> In addition, higher rates may be permitted for units previously renting for $500 or less.

> **Did You Know?**
>
> Owners of rent-stabilized units can increase their revenues by providing new services, adding new equipment, or making improvements to those apartments. This is on top of the regular annual RGB increases.
>
> As long as tenants agree (in writing) to the rent increases, owners can pass 1/40 of the cost of the improvement (including installation costs but excluding finance charges) along to tenants.
>
> The investor who spends $10,000 on a new kitchen and bathroom for a rent-stabilized unit, for example, can pass $300 of that expense to tenants via a rent increase.
>
> An order from the DHCR is not required before the owner collects this type of increase. For vacant units, the owner does not have to get either prior approval by DHCR or written consent of a tenant to collect the 1/40 increase.

The Rent Regulation Reform Act also had the following outcomes:

- It changed the definition of "succession" rights so that an apartment can be "passed down" for only a single generation without a vacancy increase.
- It broadened "luxury decontrol" to households earning more than $175,000 in two consecutive years with rents of $2,000 or more (previously, only households with incomes of $250,000 or more were subject to vacancy decontrol).
- It required tenants to pay rent into escrow in certain housing court disputes.

The laws surrounding rent stabilization in New York City seem daunting for investors. In this chapter, we'll attempt to fix that by explaining the rent regulations that affect New York's multifamily investors and their tenants and show you how to use these regulations to your advantage to develop your own winning investment strategy.

Just the Facts

Rent stabilization applies to tenants who live in buildings:

- Built before 1974 (or later if eligible for tax credits).
- Containing six or more units.
- That are *not* co-ops or condos (although tenants who moved in prior to the conversion are covered by rent stabilization).
- That are *not* owned by a nonprofit and run for charitable or educational purposes.
- Many other rights and "entitlements"

Rent-stabilized tenants are entitled to:

- Leases (an initial one when the apartment is first rented and renewals after) of one or two years (it's the tenant's choice).
- Rent increases only at lease renewal or when ordered by the NYS Division of Housing and Community Renewal (due to major capital improvements, for example).
- Lease renewal increases set forth by the NYC Rent Guidelines Board.
- Initial rent for an apartment on the basis of the previous tenant's rent plus the vacancy allowance and any increases permitted for improvements done by the owner.

The problem is that the current system of rent stabilization comes with legal ramifications that can land even the most conscientious landlords in court. Flanked by their attorneys, investors can wind up spending much time and money on these cases (many tenants are eligible for free legal representation). As you'll read throughout this book, the system also creates underlying societal and economic issues that have yet to be resolved.

Playing by the Rules

Leading the charge to ensure that both landlords and tenants follow the rules of rent stabilization is the DHCR. When property owners *don't* play by the rules, tenants file complaints with the governing body, which in turn serves the complaint to the owner, gathers evidence associated with the claim, and then issues a written order. That order is often fought over in landlord-tenant court. You'll read more about this venue and how to manage it later in this book.

When tenants prevail, the DHCR reduces rents and imposes civil penalties. If, for example, it's found that an owner has neglected to maintain services by not repainting the building's - common areas every three years (as required by law), then rents will could be reduced to offset the violation. In some cases, the DHCR will also assess interest penalties and/or treble damages payable to the tenant. (See "The Legalities of It All" section in this chapter for more information on treble damages.)

Rent Stabilization Calculations

Each year, the RGB establishes the lease guidelines for hotels, apartments, and single-room occupancies (SROs). The Rent Stabilization Law sets forth the factors that must be considered by the board prior to the adoption of rent guidelines. These include:

- The economic condition of the residential real estate industry in NYC, including such factors as the prevailing and projected (i) real estate taxes and sewer and water rates, (ii) gross operating maintenance costs (including insurance rates, governmental fees, cost of fuel, and labor charges), (iii) costs and availability of financing (including effective rates of interest), and (iv) overall supply of housing accommodations and overall vacancy rates.
- Relevant data from the current and projected cost-of-living indexes for the affected area and other RGB data.

Members of the public are invited to attend meetings and hearings held by the RGB either by testifying at hearings or by submitting written testimony. The organization holds eight to 10 meetings per year to discuss its research agenda, review staff reports, and hear testimony from invited guests, including public officials, housing experts, and industry and tenant representatives.

The Rent Stabilization Law and City Charter hold annual hearings prior to the adoption of rent guidelines. Separate hearings are held for the apartment and hotel sectors. Notice of the hearings is provided in the City Record for eight days and at least once in a newspaper of general circulation at least eight days before the hearing. The hearings are usually held in mid-June just prior to the board's July 1 deadline for promulgating new guidelines.

About one week after the final vote, the board's orders and related explanatory statements are filed with the city clerk and published in the City Record. The Rent Stabilization Law directs that the filing of the board's orders and its findings (i.e., the explanatory statements) must be completed no later than July 1 of each year.

The guidelines themselves go into effect for leases being renewed and vacancies occurring on or after October 1 of the same year and on or before September 30 of the following year. Memorizing the document won't put any more money in your pocket, but if you're having trouble sleeping at night, you might want to check out the RGB's Orders and Explanatory Statements online at http://www.housingnyc.com/downloads/guidelines/aptorders.pdf.

Rent-Controlled Calculations

In rent-controlled units, monthly rents are determined by the maximum base rent (MBR) system, which is also developed by the RGB. The rent is adjusted every two years to reflect changes in operating costs. At those intervals, owners can raise rents up to 7.5 percent annually until they hit the MBR. Tenants can stand in the way of those increases on the basis of two factors: the building is in violation of the DHCR's regulations or the owner's expenses don't warrant an increase.

The rent that the tenant ultimately pays is known as the maximum collectible rent (MCR) and increases annually until it reaches MBR, which is updated every two years. New York City Local Law 30 of 1970 stipulates that MBR be established for apartments according to a formula calculated to reflect real estate taxes, water and sewer charges, operating and maintenance expenses, return on capital value, and vacancy and collection loss allowance.

Rents can also go up as a result of the following factors:

- Higher fuel costs
- Increased labor costs
- With the occupying tenant's written consent
- An increase in services, equipment, or improvements made to the apartment (with written consent of the occupying tenant)
- Installation of a building-wide major capital improvement (with DHCR approval)
- In cases of hardship (with DHCR approval)

Only those landlords that apply for and receive an order of eligibility (an order stating that the unit is indeed eligible for a rent increase) from DHCR can increase tenants' rent.

The Legalities of It All

The most financially damaging snag that owners of rent-regulated apartments run into involves rent overcharges. Whether intentional or unintentional, these overcharges can land owners in court, where they may be ordered to refund excess rent collected on the basis of a finding of a rent overcharge. A finding by DHCR of a *willful* rent overcharge by the owner may result in the assessment of treble damages, payable to the tenant.

> **DEFINITION: TREBLE DAMAGES**
>
> Treble damages are awarded when the DHCR finds that a tenant has been overcharged for rent. To make sure its point is heard, the group imposes three times the amount of the overcharge on rent-stabilized apartments. Treble damages are imposed only if the complaint is filed less than two years after the overcharge occurred.

Another pitfall investors must avoid is the failure to provide required services and/or to make needed repairs for an individual apartment or property-wide. If, for example, a tenant complains of a lack of heat or hot water, the grievance must be handled in a timely manner. Garbage piled up in halls or other common areas and broken door or window locks also fall under this category. These issues should be common sense for all landlords.

> **DID YOU KNOW?**
>
> Rent-stabilized tenants have rights of succession, or the right to inherit an apartment, when the main tenant dies or moves and an immediate family (or family-like) member has been living in the apartment and wants to stay in it. They also have the right to organize a tenants' association and to file complaints about service and repair rights that all stabilized tenants possess. Finally, most tenants can also share and sublet their apartments (with their landlord's permission).

If not attended to, these repairs could translate into violations and subsequent penalties for the building owners. The tenant who is granted a rent reduction by the DHCR for such conditions is free from paying for any rent increases until services are restored and until the governing body reinstates the rent.

> **DID YOU KNOW?**
>
> All rent-regulated tenants can obtain a rent freeze and rent reduction if the landlord is not providing services or making repairs and the tenant follows the proper procedures. To get the rent freeze and roll back, the tenant must write a letter to the landlord, mailed by certified mail, describing the problem. If, after 10 days, the owner doesn't fix the issue, the tenant can file for a decrease with the DHCR.

The law also prohibits harassment of rent-stabilized tenants. That includes any intentional actions that are used to force a tenant to vacate an apartment. Landlords found guilty of harassment can be denied decontrol (the removal of rent stabilization for a particular unit or an entire building), fined up to $5,000 for each violation, and even slapped with both civil and criminal penalties.

The Tenants' Roles

Tenants have their own set of rules that they have to play by or risk eviction, penalties, and other sanctions. While they obviously benefit from artificially low rents and the ability to renew leases every year, tenants must use the dwellings as their primary residences. The celebrity who resides in the United Kingdom, for example, and who has an apartment in NYC can't take advantage of rent stabilization for the latter unit.

Tenants are told that they also have to take care of their apartments, despite the fact that many of them live there for decades on end in order to continue taking advantage of rent stabilization. They can be evicted for nonpayment of rent, illegal or "nuisance" behavior, violating the lease (by subletting the unit to someone else without the landlord's permission, for example), or when a landlord wants to use the unit for his or her own personal use.

Warning to investors: here's where you'll experience your first double standard in the landlord-tenant relationship. The law says that renters have to take care of their apartments and comply with other rules, but I've yet to see a single tenant evicted or have his or her rent increased due to noncompliance. But if a landlord even *looks* like he or she is breaking the law, rents can be reduced swiftly or not paid at all until the problem is rectified. Tenants have all kinds of leeway thanks to rent regulations. If you get into New York real estate and expect the landlord-tenant laws to work in your favor, then your investment returns will be disappointing. My best advice, stay out of the court system as much as possible and negotiate one on one.

As you can see, when landlords or tenants shirk their respective duties in the rental relationship, the situation can quickly turn from amicable to adversarial. In chapter 7 of this book, you'll learn how to successfully navigate landlord-tenant court and how to win the war instead of focusing on individual battles.

Should We Keep Rent Regulation?

As someone who lives, works, and breathes the NYC multifamily market on a daily basis, I can tell you that while the rules governing the environment are straightforward, the scenarios that make up the city's apartment scene are as complex as they are varied. On the one hand, rent stabilization affords an economically diverse group of citizens the chance to live in the Big Apple without breaking the bank. On the other, it has created an artificially suppressed real estate paradigm that doesn't always benefit those intended.

In Peter Salins's recent book *Scarcity by Design,* the chairman of the Department of Urban Affairs and Planning at Hunter College states that the most distressing and consistent reality of rent regulation is what we might call the "all the wrong people" syndrome.

"With almost faultless precision the rent-regulation system bypasses, or hurts, those it was meant to help, and heaps most of its benefits on relatively privileged New Yorkers," writes Salins (see Mildner and Salins 1991). "The system does not help the poor; it particularly penalizes new New Yorkers, who have always been vital to the city's economy; and it encourages landlords and tenants alike to behave in ways almost perfectly calculated to tighten the housing market still further and raise rental prices higher."

According to Salins, the abiding sin of rent control is that it misallocates resources. It is a truism, for instance, that housing in New York is expensive. But the truism is not true. "Housing in New York is cheap, or at least New York has lots of cheap housing, and average prices are reasonable," he says. "The problem is that the wrong people live in that cheap housing, while many others are stuck in housing they cannot really afford."

I walk into these rent-stabilized apartments all day long and have even owned a few. Residing in them are tenants who have become "married" to the idea that they are stuck in their apartments because of the low rent. They don't aspire to "move up," like many of their peers outside of New York City would, simply because they know they'd have to pay market rates for their dwellings. This scenario freezes tenants in time. For example:

> Let's look at the tenant who has spent the past 20 years in a rent-stabilized apartment in Manhattan and who pays $500 a month for the unit. If that unit were deregulated, it would probably fetch $2,700 a month, which means the tenant is saving $2,200 a month by staying put and not moving.
>
> But what happens when the tenant is forced to move to grab a great job opportunity in another city? For one, he or she will be ill equipped to deal with the realities of the housing market, due to that artificial economic bubble that he or she was living in. Call it Economics 101, but this tenant will have to budget for a larger rent payment, consider the fact that eviction can take place (if warranted), and factor in future rent increases.

Rent regulations hold people back, not to mention that a large portion of their beneficiaries don't truly need the financial support that it provides. New York Congressman Charles B. Rangel illegally rents multiple rent-stabilized apartments in Lenox Terrace, where he pays about half the market rate for the units. His neighbors in the complex include Governor David A. Paterson, another politician who benefits from rent regulations.

Mick Jagger's ex-wife Bianca is currently fighting to keep her rent-stabilized unit on Park Avenue. Evicted from the apartment in 2007, Jagger has been litigating for several years with the landlord over whether the unit is her primary residence.

The list of high-profile individuals who take advantage of rent stabilization is long and includes actor Mia Farrow, singer Cyndi Lauper, and supermodel Kim Alexis, to name just a few. Dignitaries, politicians, and celebrities alike are living in rent-stabilized apartments in New York City—hardly the type of people the system was meant to help in the first place.

Negative Momentum

Economists are virtually unanimous in the conclusion that rent control is destructive. In a poll of American economists in the late '70s, 98 percent agreed that "a ceiling on rents reduces the quantity and quality of housing available" (Alston et al. 1992). The agreement cuts across the usual political spectrum, ranging all the way from Nobel Prize winners Milton Friedman and Friedrich Hayek on the right to their fellow Nobel Laureate Gunnar Myrdal on the left. Swedish economist (and socialist) Assar Lindbeck (1972) asserted, "In many cases rent control appears to be the most efficient technique presently known to destroy a city—except for bombing."

That's where deregulation plays a role. Henry O. Pollakowski, a housing economist at the Massachusetts Institute of Technology's Center for Real Estate and editor of the *Journal of Housing Economics*, sees deregulation as a positive move and says traditional economic analysis suggests that when price controls (rent regulation) are imposed on housing stock, housing quality declines over time because landlords are unable to recoup their investment and routine maintenance costs.

Conversely, rent deregulation should lead to significant new investment in housing that was previously rent stabilized. History suggests that complete deregulation of stabilized dwelling units would lead to important gains in housing quality in New York. These investment gains might also lead to neighborhood "spillover" effects as owners of property proximate to buildings experiencing new investment feel more comfortable making additional investments themselves. This may be why you are reading this book.

"Given the need for better maintenance and increased renovation of New York's aging housing stock," Pollakowski (2003) concludes, "such an increase represents a considerable potential boon to the city's residents, and should draw serious consideration from New York City policymakers."

Holding Steady

Rent stabilization doesn't look to be going away anytime soon. Renters and their supporters are tied to the concept and don't want to give it up—even the folks who have since moved to Albuquerque and are now subleasing their rent-stabilized units to friends. Also clinging to the system are those who clearly benefit from it, even though they don't need the financial assistance that it provides.

I have a building listed for sale right now on 30th Street in Manhattan where one tenant is paying $800 a month for a unit that's probably worth $2,500 a month. In fact, he even spent $30,000 of his own money to upgrade the unit to his liking, (almost 2 years worth of rent). He has a $4-million home on Timberline Road in East Hampton, New York, zip 11937, but because of the way the laws are written—and because he claims that his Manhattan home is his primary residence—he can go ahead and benefit from rent stabilization. Clearly, this is not the type of person whom rent regulation was created for, but yet, to him the benefit flows.

Important Rent Regulation Terms

Deregulation: Also known as "decontrol" or "destabilization." Deregulation occurs by action of the owner when an apartment under either rent control or rent stabilization legally meets the criteria for leaving regulation. When an apartment is deregulated, the rent may be set at "market rate." There are two types of deregulation, commonly referred to as luxury decontrol (also high-income, high-rent decontrol) and vacancy decontrol (also high-rent vacancy decontrol).

Essential services: Under rent control, the owner must provide and maintain all services furnished or required to be furnished on the base date. These services are called essential services and may include but are not limited to repairs, decorating, and maintenance; the furnishing of light, heat, and hot and cold water; elevator service; kitchen, bath, and laundry facilities and privileges; janitor service; and removal of refuse. Essential services for apartments can be building-wide, such as heat, hot water, elevator service, and maintenance of public areas of the building. The service may also be something furnished within an individual apartment, such as a refrigerator, a stove, air-conditioning equipment, or painting.

Fair-market rents: In New York City, when a tenant voluntarily vacates a rent-controlled apartment, the apartment becomes decontrolled. If that apartment is in a building containing six or more units, the apartment becomes rent stabilized. The owner may charge the first stabilized tenant a fair-market rent. All future rent increases are subject to limitations under the Rent Stabilization Law, whether the same tenant renews the lease or the apartment is rented to another tenant. The Rent Stabilization Law permits the first stabilized tenant after decontrol to challenge the first rent charged after decontrol, through a Fair Market Rent Appeal (FMRA), if the tenant believes that the rent set by the owner exceeds the fair-market rent for the apartment. The appeal is decided taking into consideration the Fair Market Rent Special Guideline and rents for comparable apartments. An FMRA must be filed within 90 days after the tenant receives the initial apartment registration.

Fuel cost adjustment: The New York City Rent Control Law allows separate adjustments based on the changes, up or down, in the price of various types of heating fuels. The adjustment will be based on fuel price changes between the beginning and the end of the prior year. Only tenants in rent-controlled apartments located in New York City are subject to this fuel cost adjustment. Early rent-stabilized New York City Rent Guidelines Board orders also contained supplementary guidelines regarding the denomination of fuel cost adjustments.

Source: NYC Rent Guidelines Board (http://www.housingnyc.com/)

Is It Good for Me?

By keeping a certain percentage of New York City's apartment inventory in rent stabilization, policy makers are actually reducing the available housing stock. Let's say I owned 2,000 apartments in the city and 1,000 of them are rent stabilized. That means that my free-market rents are valid for only half of my housing stock rather than the entire 2,000 units. The law makes the nonregulated units much more expensive, penalizing new renters and "freezing" the other 1,000—giving the rent-stabilized people an artificial reason to stay.

If you removed rent stabilization altogether, the average rent for most New Yorkers would come down—maybe not to the artificially low levels that the regulation's beneficiaries were experiencing but certainly to more affable prices than are being offered now on the free market.

All this said, here is the biggest irony. For investors, the proposition of owning rent-stabilized units can be particularly compelling. In fact, such properties have been luring in a growing number of real estate investors for years. I've brokered hundreds of these transactions and have seen the positive results that come when someone selects the right property and negotiates the best possible deal.

Making the Transition

Let's say a tenant passes away or moves to another country. After some investment, the unit he or she has been renting for $700 a month can be deregulated, which means you can rent it for market rates, say, $2,100 a month. That's three times what you ever expected to bring in from that specific unit and all because the tenant is no longer able to occupy the apartment. It equates to a increase of $16,800 in rent annually that you didn't expect. Where else do you get that upside? Not Chicago.

As evidenced by the recent market downturn—and New York City's relative insulation from the real estate plunge (the vacancy rate increased from 2 to 4 percent)—factors such as scarcity of land, a thriving business environment, and steady demand for living space make the city a great investment choice.

Considering that units are deregulated almost daily, the investment case becomes even more compelling. The investor who purchases a $3-million building where 10 units are stabilized goes into the deal knowing that options are limited when it comes to rent increases and tenant selection for those apartments.

But if that same owner can find a way to get five or six of those existing renters to move out, then he or she can increase the value of the new acquisition by 40 or 50 percent. The owner has the luxury of time to make those departures happen because he or she already factored in the rent stabilization before buying the building.

So, you ask, how does this owner go about legally deregulating those 10 units? There are several techniques I've seen used successfully. He or she might offer individual tenants cash settlements for vacating the apartments while knowing that the ultimate payoff will far surpass the total amount it will take to entice the renters to leave. Soon after, that $3-million building increases in value to $4.5 or $5 million, all because a few tenants were moved around.

Lucrative Investments

Throughout this book, I'll be sharing with you top investment strategies for New York City's multifamily real estate market. You'll learn, for example, that there's real value in getting out into your buildings and into the lives of the people who are dwelling in them. Only then can you make the kind of landlord-tenant deals that result in lucrative real estate investments.

What I won't help you do is fight a rent regulation system that's been in place for decades and serves as a point of conflict for New Yorkers, politicians, attorneys, and landlords. I will help you understand the dynamics of it and how to follow in the footsteps of the many investors who are thriving in the city's multifamily market.

2
Why NYC Real Estate is Unique

> *All you have to do is look at this 50-year-old building to see that there are no penthouses, certainly not my apartment. I pay the maximum legal rent and, in fact, would be violating the law if I paid more.*
>
> —CHARLES RANGEL, CONGRESSMAN

You have to love quotations like that. In fact, he was caught breaking a few real estate laws recently. But people like this just contribute to the several factors that make the New York City real estate market unique. The city's supply and demand fundamentals play a key role in shaping the landscape, as do rent stabilization and the social implications associated with the New York City rental scene.

These factors can come together to make New York real estate a good investment, even despite the overall economic downturn and housing market declines that took hold nationwide in 2007. If you have the right investment horizon, I'll give you a look at some compelling reasons for investing in multifamily housing in New York.

Supply and Demand Fundamentals

Manhattan is an island with almost no developable land. It's six miles wide and 13 miles long, and it's not getting any bigger. That equates to high renter competition for landlords looking for the best return on their investments. People flock to the island to live, visit, and work, and in doing so they enhance investors' chances of keeping vacancy rates low. Together, these fundamentals help to create a positive investment outlook for anyone who owns property in the city. For example, talk to an apartment building owner in Florida in 2009 who woke up some mornings to discover that a tenant moved out of their units in the middle of the night. In markets like these, if you don't have a real good handle on your operations, your occupancy can go from 90%-70% in 45 days. Ironically most Manhattan landlords would be happy if their tenants left in the middle of the night.

Let's take an in-depth look at the most important fundamentals at work here:

Geographic Issues

This 78-square-mile island isn't getting any bigger. No one is making any more land. Surrounded on three sides by water, Manhattan is built out with little room for more development; that creates additional competition.

> **JUST THE FACTS**
>
> At the center of the island is Central Park, now more than 125 years old, which divides the island into quarters. The area directly south of Central Park is called "Midtown," while the area below that is called "Downtown."
>
> Everything from the middle of the park to the island's northern tip is "Uptown." The part of the island closest to Long Island is called the "East Side," and the portion nearer the Hudson River is the "West Side." The two neighborhoods lying on either side of Central Park are called the "Upper East Side" and the "Upper West Side."

Compare this to the investor who is looking to buy an apartment building somewhere where land is plentiful. That prospective landlord has to look at what properties his or hers will compete with both now and in the future. New York City landlords don't have to stress over such things because the chances of someone putting up a skyscraper on the lot next door are possible but very costly, difficult, and, in most cases, not probable.

Vacancies Are Few

Even if a new building goes up in the city, your competitor won't suck up all of your rental demand, anyway, because so many people want to live in New York. This 24-hour international city is hard for people to resist, hence the constant influx of both American and foreign-born individuals to New York.

VACANT UNITS AVAILABLE FOR RENT BY BOROUGH NEW YORK CITY 2005 AND 2008

Borough	Vacant Units Available for Rent		Net Vacancy Rate[a]	
	2005	2008	2005	2008
Total	64,737	61,762	3.09%	2.88%
Bronx[b]	9,952	11,836	2.63	3.07
Brooklyn	17,759	15,530	2.78	2.34
Manhattan[b]	22,198	16,110	3.79	2.70
Queens	12,239	14,707	2.82	3.32
Staten Island	(c)	(c)	(c)	6.37[d]

Sources: U.S. Bureau of the Census, 2005 and 2008 New York City Housing and Vacancy Surveys.

Notes:
[a] The vacancy rate is calculated by dividing vacant available for rent units that are not dilapidated by the sum of vacant available for rent units that are not dilapidated and renter-occupied units. The standard error of the vacancy rate for all renter units in the city in 2008 was 0.16 percent.
[b] Marble Hill included in The Bronx.
[c] The New York City Housing and Vacancy Survey is a sample survey. The number of vacant units available for rent in this category is too small to report.
[d] The number of vacant units available for rent in this category is small, interpret with caution.

According to the Rent Guidelines Board (RGB), between 2005 and 2008, the rental vacancy rate in Manhattan decreased from 3.79 to 2.70 percent. The rates in the Bronx and Queens were 3.07 and 3.32 percent, respectively, in 2008, while they were 2.63 and 2.82 percent, respectively, in 2005. The rate in Brooklyn was 2.34 percent in 2008, while it was 2.78 percent in 2005 (compare this to national vacancy rates for apartment properties, which were 7.2 percent in commercial real estate firm Grubb and Ellis's most recent report).

Just the Facts

In February 2009, the city's Department of Housing Preservation and Development reported that there were 1,027,000 rent-stabilized units (occupied and vacant), comprising 47.9 percent of the rental stock in 2008. The number of rent-stabilized units decreased by 17,000, or by 1.6 percent, in the three years between 2005 and 2008.

The number of owner units, occupied and vacant together, was 1,046,000, or 31.4 percent of the housing inventory in the city, in 2008.

With occupancy rates in the 97 to 99 percent range for years in New York City, you have excessive renter demand and limited supply. In essence, in a housing shortage, the winners are the property owners, who aren't subjected to the massive fluctuations in vacancy rates that investors experience in other suburban areas.

NYC Apartments Wanted

Jonathan Miller, author of the Urban Land Institute and PricewaterhouseCoopers' "Emerging Trends" report, called the multifamily market "the only real investment opportunity of 2009," as the credit crunch continued to steer people away from home ownership.

Investors of all types are cashing in on the trend. Deals closed in 2009 included a $54-million Upper Manhattan multifamily portfolio consisting of 500 units throughout 21 walk-up buildings, a $58-million portfolio of 10 multifamily buildings in the Inwood and Washington Heights sections of Manhattan, the $38-million sale of five Brooklyn multifamily properties, and a $277-million portfolio of multifamily properties.

> As one city investor summed it up, the multifamily product "is, and always has been, highly sought after primarily due to the safety of the investment owing to the artificially low rent levels that are created by rent regulation . . . the higher the percentage of rent regulated units in a building, the more interest is generated from the marketplace."

Companies Gravitate to NYC

The latest U.S. Census numbers indicate that more than eight million people now live in New York City, the most in the city's history. Companies continue to use the region as a place to set up headquarters, according to the Department of City Planning (DCP), which anticipates a need to accommodate more than 440,000 new workers by 2025 (see below).

> **JUST THE FACTS**
>
> The list of corporations with headquarters in New York City includes (but isn't limited to):
>
> - Citigroup
> - CBS Corporation
> - Bank of America
> - Dow Jones & Company
> - Bristol-Myers Squibb
> - Metropolitan Life Insurance Company
> - Sirius Satellite Radio
> - Random House
> - Redken
> - MTV
> - Steinway & Sons
> - Tiffany & Co.
> - Time Warner
> - Verizon Communications
>
> *continues* ▶

- Veronis Suhler Stevenson
- Viacom
- The list goes on . . .

Despite gloomy forecasts about the national economy, Mayor Michael R. Bloomberg is holding firm to a bold promise to "create or save" 400,000 jobs in the city over the next six years. The people holding those jobs will need homes.

Increasingly, people are moving into Manhattan to be closer to work and to feed off of Midtown's cultural and entertainment energy. "The demand for new housing in New York City is great and is expected to grow," says the DCP (2010), which estimates a need of 12,600 new housing units by 2025 to accommodate the influx of new residents into Manhattan.

According to Rosemary Scanlon, a consultant in urban and regional economics, population growth since 2000 and the strong post-2003 economy have put additional pressure on New York's already scarce housing supply.

Doing Business in a Cultural Mecca

I have a client whose family, in fleeing the Holocaust, wound up in South America. They all learned to speak Spanish fluently, not knowing how valuable the language would be when they came to New York City. A cultural Mecca, the city is composed of many different cultures, many of which rely on Spanish as their first language.

My client successfully owned and rented out buildings in the Bronx, where Spanish-speaking tenants were prevalent. He gained a competitive advantage because he could speak to them in their own tongues and handle questions and complaints quickly, without the need for an interpreter.

He recently sold his entire rental portfolio for $300 million.

The demand is reflected in the number of building permits issued for residential construction—up from levels of 15,000 units per year in 2000–2002 to 30,000 units per year in 2005–2007. "Demand has pushed up prices for condominiums, co-ops, and rentals in Manhattan and Brooklyn," says Scanlon (see Scanlon and Cohen 2008). "Rents in stabilized buildings have continued to rise as well."

Multifamily Units in High Demand

Multifamily apartment buildings are in high demand in New York City, where such units have historically yielded good investments because of artificially low rental rates created by rent regulation (see "Different from the Rest of the World" section below).

Those buildings with a high percentage of regulated units are considered as safe as bond investments, yet they yield equity-like returns over time. These buildings attract renters: the higher the number of rent-regulated units within a structure, the more interest from the existing renter pool. Combine these attributes and you end up with an investment that yields impressive returns over time, if purchased correctly.

> **NOTABLE QUOTES**
>
> "Demand for affordable housing in New York City is overwhelming; it always has been and it always will be," said Deborah VanAmerongen, commissioner of the State Division of Housing and Community Renewal (see Murray 2009).

Different from the Rest of the World

Buying a multifamily property in New York City is a unique experience. Rent regulations create an artificial scarcity of market rate units that landlords in other cities don't benefit from. Not only is it difficult for renters to find available apartments but also the price of "open" units may be inflated because of the rental price caps on rent-stabilized dwellings.

The situation could tighten up further over the coming years. According to a 2008 study by economist Rosemary Scanlon (and commissioned by the Manhattan Institute), "Rising costs, driven by steep increases in the costs of materials, land and labor, and the delays and resulting high costs of the local permitting and regulatory process, pose a threat to constructing housing that is affordable for low- and middle-income New Yorkers" (see Scanlon and Cohen 2008).

Did You Know?

The New York State Housing Finance Agency (HFA) recently issued revised allocation criteria for developers seeking private activity tax-exempt bond financing for so-called 80/20 multifamily rental projects in New York City.

To qualify for an allocation of private activity bonds, or volume cap, developers of 80/20 multifamily rental projects must agree to set aside 20 percent of the units for low-income households with incomes at or below 50 percent of the area median income (AMI) or 25 percent of units for households with incomes at or below 60 percent of AMI. The current AMI in New York City for a family of four is $59,700.

HFA is allocating up to $1 billion in volume cap over the next three years for New York City 80/20 multifamily rental projects. About $400 million has already been committed, leaving $600 million available for new commitments.

The same can't be said for markets such as Houston and Los Angeles, where market demand dictates how much a unit will rent for. Rent regulation creates a different environment. According to William Tucker, author of *The Excluded Americans: Homelessness and Housing Policies and Zoning, Rent Control and Affordable Housing*, cities where rent regulations exist usually possess two housing markets: the market in which prices are held down via the regulations and a "shadow" market in which prices skyrocket. In cities such as Atlanta or Chicago, for example, where there are no rent regulations, the housing market is moderately priced. In New York City, it is not.

Where Rent Stabilization Comes In

In chapter 1, you learned about the origin of rent stabilization, why it was enacted, and how it works. The main point you took away from the chapter was the fact that rent stabilization has played—and continues to play—a key role in the city's multifamily real estate market. In this section, we'll further explore the concept and learn how it can benefit you as an investor.

A Layer of Security

Rent stabilization insulates investors from the impact of major job losses, for example, because renters are already paying a lower than market rent for their units. Even major economic shifts have little effect on the rent-stabilized owner's cash flow, which is artificially low to begin with.

> **DID YOU KNOW?**
>
> Democrats now control the state legislature and intend to revive some of the rent control laws that have been liberalized over the past few decades. The legislation would move thousands of previously deregulated apartments back under regulation; reduce allowed rent increase percentages, even when a tenant moves out; limit an owner's ability to use his or her regulated apartments for personal use; and crack down on harassment of tenants by landlords to induce eviction. A New York investor needs to be constantly aware of local and state politics.

Steady Rental Stream

When you purchase a New York City apartment building that's full of rent-stabilized tenants, you're buying into an environment where average rents in the building are typically about 50 percent of the actual monthly price of renting those apartments in a free market. That provides a significant layer of security for the landlord, who can operate mostly unaffected by decreases in "market rent" when economic issues such as major corporate layoffs occur. In this case, if a tenant loses a job and must move out of a rent-stabilized apartment, the landlord could actually benefit! In fact, the landlord just got a gift because rent on that unit will most likely now increase by more than 30 percent.

The same doesn't hold true in a city such as Dallas, where apartments renting for $700 a month likely sat vacant for long spells in the wake of the Enron scandal and subsequent shutdown. Desperate owners who dropped the price of their units to $600 to compensate also took a big hit on both asset value and cash flow generation.

Buy a building in New York where free-market apartments go for $2,200 a month and rent-stabilized units fetch $1,110 a month, however, and you wind up feeling much less impact when the financial services industry takes a big hit and closes up some of its Wall Street offices. Market rents may drop, but at the same time, rent-stabilized tenants begin paying $1,150 because of a legislated rent increase. See the difference? Stabilization acts as a hedge.

Equity Returns for Bond Risks

Even as the rest of the United States experienced steep housing market declines in the late 2000s, New York City's multifamily market held its own. From 2007 to 2008, for example, the value of apartment buildings was down an average of just 5 percent. Although snother - decrease would follow in 2009, this was modest compared to the devastation many Americans witnessed in their stock portfolios and retirement accounts.

Credit the factors outlined earlier in this chapter with helping to create an environment that's attractive to individual, portfolio, and institutional investors alike. According to the most recent numbers, the average capitalization rate for multifamily properties has inched up from an average of 5.5 percent in the first half of 2007 to 5.8 percent. Even today, they are on par with the cost of debt.

Maintaining Their Value

Real estate experts expected financial and real estate markets to bottom in 2009 and then falter for much of 2010, with continued drops in property values and additional foreclosures and delinquencies, according to the 2009 "Emerging Trends in Real Estate" report, released by the Urban Land Institute and PricewaterhouseCoopers.

But there are a few bright spots in this rather gloomy forecast. At the top of the list: apartments, which the firm calls "the best opportunity investment."

"Even though there is a lot of doom and gloom in terms of the fundamentals, interviewees really believe that 2009 is a great time to buy," says Susan Smith, director in the real estate business advisory services group at New York City–based PricewaterhouseCoopers (http://www.pwc.com). "The number-one buy is apartments. One of the main reasons why is the very diverse economic and demographic demand for apartments, especially for transit-oriented housing." This is why I mention you have to be in this game for the long haul. Don't play if you want your money back in 3 years. If you can wait 10, keep reading.

Rent-stabilized units in New York City are expected to fare particularly well, namely, as a result of the mix of low rents and market rents that landlords who own them can command. High occupancy rates sweeten the case even further, making multifamily investment a win-win scenario for investors.

It's for Tenants, Right?

Rent stabilization is supposed to help tenants, correct? Not always. In fact, it virtually freezes many of them in time, holding them in a stage of life that they can't break out of because their rents are so cheap that moving becomes the unthinkable.

> ### Social Implications
>
> If you give something to people for free, they have a tendency to take it for granted and not respect it. For those with children, you know, that without working for their allowances, your offspring will come to expect something for nothing. I guess this is part of human nature.
>
> I walked through a 400-unit HUD property near JFK Airport the other day and couldn't believe my eyes. Could it really be that the able-bodied 17- to 30-year-old tenants who occupied the building were lying around playing video games on their computers and televisions all day? And—even worse—that they were throwing their household trash out into the courtyard to avoid having to walk down the hallway to use a garbage chute?
>
> These people were clearly capable of picking up after themselves, but they were inside playing video games all day. They were given housing for free and weren't being productive with their time. They showed no consideration for their own environment because it didn't mean anything to them. This is the dark underbelly that occurs when you have people taking advantage of significant government handouts; it manifests itself in ugly ways. In fact, this handout acts as a "disincentive" to going out and finding legitimate work, because once that income is shown, the tenant will no longer be eligible for the government handout.

Did You Know?

HUD. When I refer to a property being "HUD", that is industry shorthand describing a situation where tenants receive subsidies for the majority, if not the entirety of their rent. While some landlords like this regular cash flow, it comes with its own set of regulations, property maintenance requirements, and tenant personalities to deal with.

Sorry to say but the scenario is real and is playing out on a daily basis all over the city, thanks to rent stabilization laws. We will further examine the social implications of rent stabilization and look at some of the negative factors associated with this unfortunate way of legislating housing stock

---

So, who is rent stabilization really designed to help? Certainly not the tenant who, back in 1991, started paying $800 a month for a rent-stabilized unit. Over time, that rent increased to $1,300 a month, and while that's still much lower than the free-market rent that the apartment would command, that tenant has missed out considerably by not shelling out a $25,000 deposit 18 years ago to own a unit that today is probably worth about $750,000.

Just the Facts

The beneficiaries of [the rent regulation] system often consider their rent-controlled apartment a lifetime entitlement and even count it as an asset. They form tenant groups. They pressure the city and state governments. So do the builders who want to end the laws, but they have not been as successful. The politicians understand there are more votes in tenants than in owners in New York City.

Source: Gregory Bresiger, *Housing Socialism Part II* (2006)

The tenant may have been paying cheap rent all those years, but he or she also missed out on an incredible wealth generator: homeownership. Instead, the tenant bought into the idea that rent stabilization was in place to protect him or her and ignored the fiscal advantages of taking out a mortgage and purchasing a New York

City property. My partner Joe Koicim has often said that many landlords he speaks to call it "legal stealing."

> **DID YOU KNOW?**
>
> Rents serve two functions essential to the efficient operation of housing markets:
>
> - They compensate providers of existing housing units and developers of new units for the cost of providing shelter to consumers.
> - They provide the economic incentives needed to attract new investment in rental housing, as well as to maintain existing housing stock. In this respect, housing is no different from other commodities, such as food and clothing: the amount that producers supply is directly related to the prevailing market price.
>
> Microeconomics experts understand the supply/demand consequence of price controls: a decrease in the supply of a good and, thus, shortages at the prescribed price. However, rent regulation is more than just a price control; its effects compound over time.
>
> **Source:** National Multi Housing Council (http://www.nmhc.org/)

Discouraging Homeownership

New York City's homeownership rate is half of the national average, proof that rent stabilization discourages tenants from purchasing homes. The homeownership rate for the city as a whole was 32.9 percent in 2008 (down slightly from 33.3 percent in 2005), or one in three households, compared to a national homeownership rate of 68.1 percent. Between 2005 and 2008, the number of owner-occupied units increased by 9,000, yet during the same period, the number of all occupied units increased by 64,000, including 55,000 renter-occupied units.

For investors who are interested in taking ownership of New York City real estate, that low homeownership rate equates to even more rent competition for available properties—yet another advantage of rent stabilization for investors.

> **NOTABLE QUOTES**
>
> In a report on New York City's housing gap, Peter D. Salins, professor of urban affairs and planning, Hunter College, and senior fellow, Center for Civic Innovation, said: "New York's rent, zoning, development and environmental regulations and its other housing policies hobble all four components of a vital housing market—they keep new housing from being built, they provide disincentives to maintenance and reinvestment, they freeze much of the household population in place, and they keep obsolete housing from being removed" (Salins 1996).

Rent Regulations Lead to Tenant Stagnancy

Richard L. Cravatts, director of Boston University's Program in Book and Magazine Publishing at the Center for Professional Education, writes frequently on housing issues and says rent regulations have failed society on many fronts. "Not only has it consistently failed to serve those very individuals it was designed to help," says Cravatts, "but [rent regulations have] a number of *perverse* effects, namely, of actually creating a scarcity of affordable housing; speeding the deterioration of existing rental stock; depriving owners of constitutionally protected property rights; creating strong disincentives for new development; and skewing the marketplace with artificially high and low rent levels" (Cravatts 2003).

> **NOTABLE QUOTES**
>
> "For the 70 or 80 years of various rent- and price-control experiments, New York City has been run by liberal Democrats or moderate city Republicans, who rarely offer a dramatically different philosophy. Both local political parties usually pledge never to touch rent controls. The laws have been administered since the early 1980s by the state. And despite occasional promises to the contrary by upstate Republicans, rent controls show no signs of being eliminated." —Gregory Bresiger (2006), New York business writer and frequent contributor to the *New York Post*

Cravatts points out that rent regulations fail to assist those groups—the poor and the elderly—it was designed to help because the absence of any form of means testing and a general fear of lower-income tenants encourages landlord to "rent their controlled units to people with higher incomes and more secure lifestyles" (Cravatts 2003).

A Department of Housing and Urban Development study supported that same conclusion when it suggested that "the benefits of rent control are poorly targeted" and that "significant numbers of well-to-do renters live in rent-controlled apartments and enjoy substantial benefits, while many lower-income renters receive little or no benefit" (NMHC 2009).

"Married" to Their Apartments

It's hard to give up something that's cheap and convenient, even if improving yourself means "moving up" to a new home, a new area, or a new job. Many renters living in regulated units don't see things that way and instead choose to become "married" to their apartments for fear they won't be able to afford to live anywhere else.

Greg Bresiger, a New York business writer and frequent contributor to the *New York Post*, says rent regulations, much like every other government-instituted price control, "go against the innate human desire for improvement." Consider someone who never expects to own anything and plans to always labor for a living. "Would this person want to take a job in which his salary could be frozen or strictly controlled by a government commission?" Bresiger asks. "Not very likely" is his response (Bresiger 2006).

Most people want to succeed at what they do, whether it involves an investment, a job, or a piece of property, says Bresiger, and most people want the highest salary, the best returns on their investments, and the highest rent on their property. "No one wants an artificially imposed government limitation on his financial success," he adds. "What person accepts less money than he could have received? There is a human instinct for self-improvement—for a better life for a person and his loved ones. Why expect property owners to be any different from anyone else?" (Bresiger 2006).

Just Ask Rangel

Rent-stabilized units aren't just for the poor and the underserved, as New York Congressman Charles Rangel has proven. As one New York resident and online blogger says, "How likely is it that Congressman Rangel heads a low-income family? His net worth is somewhere between $566k and $1.2 million. Not Bill Gates worthy but certainly not low income. How did Rangel come to acquire not just one rent-stabilized apartment, but four? Certainly there is some sort of income requirements in order to qualify for rent-stabilized apartments? Nope. Actually there isn't. So how does one acquire one of these coveted apartments? There are three ways that one acquires a rent-stabilized apartment: inheritance, by knowing someone, or by paying what is referred to as 'key money' (which, while illegal, is not uncommon). And so how likely is it that low-income families acquire rent-stabilized apartments through these means? Almost never."

Penalizing Newcomers

The rent regulation system, based on the idea that there is not enough housing in the free market, becomes a kind of "vicious circle," according to Bresiger. For example, he says, there is not enough housing for middle-income and low-income people in New York City. While new buildings generally are not threatened, there is always the threat that a building will come under controls. "Indeed, in wartime there is a real potential for controls, especially in places with a long history of such rules such as New York City," warns Bresinger (2006).

As a result, few builders risk capital on low- or moderate-income units in New York unless they're privy to tax breaks. "Since most builders can't or won't play this political game, fewer units are built than if there were a free market," says Bresiger (2006). This creates a housing vacuum that penalizes newcomers (who don't usually have access to rent-stabilized units) and limits the natural supply of new housing that's available in other U.S. urban areas.

Turnover rates for rent-regulated units are low, thus creating an even bigger challenge for a new tenant who is looking for housing in the city. "Even if the building is collapsing, why leave an apartment when one is paying below-market rates?" asks Bresiger. "At the same time, why should an owner put any extra money into a property he doesn't control and on which he may be losing money?

The losers are owners and those who don't enjoy the privilege of a rent-controlled building. All this, of course, means it becomes more difficult for those looking for an apartment" (Bresiger 2006).

Peter D. Salins (1996) calls rent regulation the "granddaddy and arch villain of New York's regulatory ensemble" because it keeps the price of rental housing below market levels and allows tenants to remain in their apartments as long as they like, regardless of their landlord's wishes. Keeping prices as low as possible doesn't—in the case of rent stabilization—even result in very low prices; New York's stabilized rents are higher than most cities' unregulated ones.

"But stabilized prices are almost always the *wrong* prices, *prices* different from what an unregulated housing market would charge; and rent regulation has its most egregious impact on the middle and upper end of the market, where the price differential between market and regulated rents is greatest," says Salins (1996).

This has two undesirable effects: it reduces the demand for new housing, and it misallocates the existing housing stock. If regulated tenants in Manhattan, Riverdale, or Forest Hills moved to newer, better apartments—or bought them— the increment of additional rent or carrying costs they would have to pay would far exceed the increment of housing improvement, says Salins.

"This demand factor is more important than the prospect of future regulated rents in discouraging construction of new middle and high priced housing," says Salins. "At the same time the cessation of movement among the musical chairs exacerbates shortages in the low end of the stock, shortages that cannot be responded to by private housing suppliers because of the costs of regulation, and the incomes of the low-end tenants" (Salins 1996).

Opportunities Abound

You now know why the New York City real estate market is unique and how it can both hurt and help the tenants living there and the investors who own the buildings that those tenants live in.

Rent regulations are clearly at the center of that uniqueness in the way they dictate and affect residents and property owners. Equivalent to government price fixing, rent stabilization creates an artificial scarcity that helps building owners but deprives the residents living in those structures. As an investor it is very difficult to change the laws, so lets work on using them so you can profit.

3

Breakdown of the Multifamily Market

Wall Street accounts for only about 6 percent of the jobs in New York but 25 percent of the economic activity. Every time there's an uptick in bonuses, there's an uptick in the real estate market.

—Jonathon Miller, actor and producer

Without a solid grasp of the three categories of opportunities that make up the New York City multifamily real estate market, investors can quickly become confused and unsure of themselves. Unlike many other U.S. urban markets, the New York City market is made up of three distinct types of investment opportunities: owner occupied, low income, and luxury.

In this chapter, we'll break down the three categories and provide you with the information you need to successfully navigate some or all of them. We'll start by showing you what can happen if you ignore this very important aspect of New York City real estate investment.

Don't Go Blind

Look at sales data for New York buildings without knowledge of the market's three components and you'll be completely confused. Ignore the details behind each transaction and the confusion will grow to the point where you question your ability to compete in this market and your own investment strategy. You won't understand the sale itself, why the building sold, or what it even sold for. You'll think investors are out of their minds for paying what they did or that sellers are crazy for leaving so much money on the table.

> **WORDS TO KNOW**
>
> **Cap rate:** A measure of the ratio between the net operating income produced by an asset and its capital cost (the original price paid to buy the asset) or, alternatively, its current market value.
>
> **Price per square foot:** Determined by dividing the total price or rent by the total square footage of a unit or building.
>
> **Gross rent multiplier:** A number that when multiplied by the gross income from real property provides the value of the property.

Avoid this confusion by learning what went on behind the scenes with the transaction. Go beyond the cap rate, price per square foot, and gross multiplier, none of which tell the real story behind the deal. (Although they are all important data points, they are just snapshots in time.) Peel back a few layers and ask yourself: what was the *real* story behind this transaction?

Here's an example:

> Let's say someone purchased an owner (user occupied) building for a price that was 22 times the rent roll and that the purchase yielded a 0 percent investment return. To the uninitiated, the purchase seems ridiculous. Who would possibly want to buy a multifamily property for more than it's worth and for such a low return?
>
> Look a little closer and you'll see that the investor's game plan may have been to create an owner's duplex, improve the

garden, and relocate one rent-stabilized tenant to a new home in order to combine two units into a single unregulated apartment. Once those steps have been taken, the building's value possibly increases threefold, making a future sale extremely profitable for the investor—and all the while, the cash flow was meager.

Without having at least a cursory knowledge of the top-level housing categories, you won't be able to get to the bottom of the deal to figure out whether it's going to be lucrative. Get the story before you jump into the game and your chances for success will increase.

Now let's get into the three segments and the similarities and differences among them.

The Owner/User Route

Alistair Economakis is the perfect example of a real estate investor with an eye on the owner side of the city's market. A few years ago, he and his wife, Catherine, acquired a 15-unit rent-stabilized building at 47 East 3rd Street for $1.3 million and then set out to transform it into a five-story mansion for his family.

The plan didn't go over well with tenants, who included Janet Dunson, an actress and 15-year resident. Still, Economakis pressed on with his intention of gutting the 104-year-old tenement in order to create a five-bedroom, six-bathroom private home for himself and his wife, as well as their infant child and live-in nanny. The home would include a private gym, library, home study area, play area, den, dining room, two-story living room, and master bedroom suite that would take up most of the fourth floor.

> ### Just the Facts
>
> The owner-occupancy rule states that an owner can terminate a rent-stabilized tenant's lease if the owner provides a termination notice between 90 and 150 days before a lease expires. The landlord must use the rental space as his or her own or an immediate family member's primary residence for at least three years. After that time, the building owner can move out and rent the unit(s) for market rents.

On Economakis' side was a provision in the rent stabilization code that allows owners to take over rent-regulated apartments for their own occupancy. The law says that owners may acquire "one or more apartments" for use by themselves or a family member, which meant Economakis would have to evict 24 residents from the remaining 11 rent-stabilized apartments, at the time renting for between $500 and $1,000 a month.

When asked whether he felt turning an 11,600-square-foot tenement into a single-family dwelling was excessive, Economakis told the press: "As long as an owner can prove he has a good-faith intent to occupy the space, no one should tell him whether he has the right to live in a certain size home. Fundamentally, it's a question of who is better entitled to reside in the property, the tenants or the owner. I obviously believe the owner has the right to reside in the property he owns" (see Ferguson 2005).

> **DID YOU KNOW?**
>
> The rent stabilization law states that owner dwellings must be titled under the owner's name (such as Peter Von Der Ahe, not Peter Von Der Ahe LLC). There are certain legal liabilities that you will want to explore, however, before proceeding with a building purchase under your own name. Consult an experienced attorney.
>
> Only one of the individual owners of a building can take possession of one or more dwelling units for personal or immediate family use and occupancy, even if the building is jointly owned by two or more individuals.

After some legal wrangling that included a preliminary injunction barring the new owners from terminating the leases of five tenants, as well as various appeals, Economakis prevailed—as he should have! This is America, right? The whole project was hotly debated across a number of public venues for about three years, but in the end, it proved the strength of the rent stabilization law's "owner occupancy" rule.

The court determined that the owner's case was valid, on the basis of these three factors:

1. Many single-family homes in the city are the same size as the owner's building.

2. This is the only building that the owners own as individuals, rather than through a corporation.
3. The owners didn't want to provide separate facilities within the building for themselves and their tenants and then be concerned about disturbing tenants when the owners entertained.

As an investor, Economakis prevailed by creating a property type that holds the highest value in New York City: a single-family home. He used one of the only legal methods for converting rent-stabilized apartments (without the renters' consent) to create a home whose value now far surpasses its original price and rent-stabilized income stream. When completed, this building, now a single-family home, is worth anywhere from $1,200 to $1,800 per square foot. Not a bad profit but it didn't come easily.

Landlord Beware

Never underestimate the power of a New York City tenant, particularly when it comes to rent stabilization and eviction. A few years ago, a colleague of mine purchased a building on West 95th Street in Manhattan. He and his wife were expecting twins at the time and wanted to combine one apartment with an adjoining studio for their new additions.

The tenant living in that studio apartment spoke perfect English at the building and when she had to interact with the new owners in her unit, but she quickly lost that ability when it came time to start the eviction proceedings in landlord-tenant court. Turns out in the courtroom she spoke only Thai. New York City is required to provide interpreters for landlord-tenant proceedings, and within the entire New York legal system, there are only one or two interpreters for that language.

Just scheduling the interpreter took 16 months and basically hamstrung the new owners. They wound up paying about $50,000 in legal fees and settling out of court for an additional $50,000. It was a case where the new owners had a 100 percent legitimate reason for taking over an additional unit in their apartment under the owner-occupancy law but still got delayed and overcharged by the legalities of the process.

As an investor, you must be prepared for such scenarios. Be ready to open up your wallet and get the process moving in the right direction.

There are some limitations to the owner-occupancy rule. They are:

1. An owner cannot evict a tenant from a rent-stabilized apartment in NYC if the tenant or the spouse of the tenant is a senior citizen, 62 years or older, or is a disabled person, unless the owner provides an equivalent or superior apartment at the same or lower rent in a nearby area.
2. An owner cannot evict a tenant from a rent-stabilized apartment outside of NYC or a rent-controlled apartment statewide when a member of the household lawfully occupying the apartment is a senior citizen, 62 years or older; is a disabled person; or is any person who has been a tenant in the building for 20 years or more.

The tenants themselves can also erect barriers by fighting back against any plan to turn an apartment into an owner-occupied dwelling. If this happens, you'll need to demonstrate to the court that you're serious about living in the home and that you're not just using the law to deregulate the building's units. You may need to show architectural drawings or other proof of your plans in order to demonstrate your intentions.

Under One Roof

Robert and Cortney Novogratz know a thing or two about investing in the New York City real estate market. For the past decade or so, through a series of townhouse renovations in downtown Manhattan, these self-made and self-taught investors have bought, built, remade, and decorated once-distressed or condemned properties.

In the past 12 years, the couple has purchased somewhere in the neighborhood of 10 rundown buildings in New York City—one a former gun shop riddled with its very own bullet holes—and turned them into eclectic works of art worth millions. They've traveled the world in search of just the right touches of wrought iron sculpture and visited local flea markets for cast-off stained glass windows or the perfect mantel clock to complement the cheerful yet practical designs they create in each of their homes, which they often live in before selling.

In 1996, for example, the couple found a condemned, mid-nineteenth-century brick town house on West 19th Street and bought it with owner financing for $450,000. They gutted and rebuilt it and then rented out rooms, and then whole floors, to friends. Singer Suzanne Vega was the first official tenant, taking three floors for a few years.

> In 1998, the Novogratzes used the equity from the house to buy a manufacturing building on Thompson Street, which came with a parking lot, for nearly $500,000. They remade the manufacturing building as a home and built a new house on the lot. A few years later, the two buildings sold for almost $7 and $3.825 million, respectively.
>
> Concurrently, the pair bought and renovated four more houses on Centre Market Place in Little Italy, sold two, lived in one, and rented the fourth. In 2007, the family (which includes the Novogratzes' six children) was still living in one of the houses on Centre Market Place when they purchased a lot with a shuttered S&M club on the West Side Highway for $4.3 million. They planned to raze the place and build there, but a few months later, they received an offer from a neighbor to buy the property for $23 million. The offer was too good to refuse.

The extra effort will be worth it because the New York City properties currently selling for the highest prices per square foot are the single-family residences. We're seeing a trend throughout Manhattan, Brooklyn, and other expensive neighborhoods where owners are "taking back" their properties from rent-stabilized tenants and, in doing so, are upping their homes' value in ways not previously attainable.

The owner-occupancy route is one of the greatest investment opportunities that exists in the city, regardless of the economic conditions or the state of the housing market. It's as easy as purchasing a property, combining units (via tenant buyouts, for example), fixing it up, and putting it on a platter for a retail buyer who doesn't know about real estate investing but who likes the idea of buying a building to live in for $1,000 a square foot with rental income, instead of purchasing a condo for $1,500 a foot. The investment return can go as high as 25 percent, compared to a typical 6–8 percent.

One of the Bronfmans found this out a few years ago when he purchased a building on East 66th Street for $4 million from a nonprofit organization. After restoring the five-story, 30-foot-wide structure to single-family status, the owner sold the building to a hedge fund manager for $33 million in 2007—a decent profit.

> ### The Duplex Option
>
> If turning multiple units in a building into a single-family home isn't an option, you should consider transforming the structure into a duplex or a three-unit home.
>
> Keep the transformed structure to five units or fewer and the project will qualify for residential financing, which means you'll be able to borrow more money on it.

By recapturing a home's original glory as a single-family residence, investors can quadruple the value of their investments. The key is to look at what the building itself costs; how much in damages, expenses, and time you'll have to spend to legally remove the tenants; and how much money it will take to physically return the home to its single-family status. The latter option gets costly, particularly for buildings that have been chopped into 10 or more different units over the years.

Find a way to do it right and you'll unlock a tremendous amount of real estate value and tap into one of the greatest wealth creation facilities available in the New York City market: the arbitrage between the investment property and the "owner-user" property. It can easily translate into a 25 percent premium in price. For a property worth millions of dollars, that's an additional $250,000 for every million in value.

Low-Income Options

Known as "affordable housing," "workforce housing," or "C-class" housing, the low-income sector has stood out as a "darling" investment in New York City over the past decade. In high demand and always encompassing a rent-stabilized component, this type of housing fills a void left behind by a lack of land and a high demand for housing in general throughout the city.

Low-income housing is prevalent in areas such as Harlem, West Harlem, Hamilton Heights, Washington Heights, Brooklyn, Queens, and the Bronx. When investing in such areas, the game plan should be to use the rent stabilization laws outlined in chapter 1 of this book to your advantage. There is a housing shortage in New York, and rents in these neighborhoods have nowhere to go but up, but the strategy is different from other neighborhoods in the city.

Heard on the Street

New York has long been a target of humorous comments by comedians. On a recent episode of the TV show *30 Rock*, lead character Jack Donaghy made the comment that "since Mayor Giuliani left, it's gotten really hard to harvest hobo organs."

There's no doubt that before Giuliani came into office, many low-income neighborhoods were dangerous and crime ridden. For now at least, that situation has changed for the better: much of New York is safe, and that has opened these areas up for a wider group of investors unlike any other time in the city's history.

The investment case becomes compelling when you acquire a building where families are living in rent-stabilized units for $700 a month. Get just one of those families to move out, fix up the apartment, and rent it out for $2,200 in free-market rent and your investment return will be significant on that unit. Turn over five of those units per year and, over the course of three years, this income and the building's value will jump significantly.

In New York City, some real estate professionals refer to the low-income market as the "true investment market" because it's more similar to any other city's standard multifamily market. The buildings sell on income and the ability to increase rents, as opposed to the owner-user transactions discussed earlier in this chapter, which find investors buying property that may not generate much cash flow but will increase in value when certain steps are taken.

With "low-income" property, you'll make your profit in two ways: through cash flow and via appreciation. By exploiting the rent stabilization rules, you'll purchase buildings that have average rents that are lower than the typical monthly costs of renting a deregulated unit, and you can use tenant turnovers, the creation of vacancies, and tools such as J-51 property tax exemptions to increase the property's income stream.

The tax break system isn't always easy to navigate, as Tishman Speyer Properties recently learned. In cases where landlords make significant building renovations, they are allowed to pass along a portion of the renovation costs to the tenants' rent. As a result, landlords can raise rents that exceed or approach the $2,000 deregulation threshold.

The Lowdown on J-51 Exemptions

New York City provides owners of residential buildings with tax incentives to rehabilitate these buildings. After doing certain categories of rehabilitation work, owners are eligible to receive a J-51 property tax abatement and/or a J-51 property tax exemption.

Here's the difference between the two programs:

- **A J-51 property tax abatement** reduces the amount of taxes owed by the building owner by an amount tied to the cost of the work done.
- **A J-51 property tax exemption** effectively freezes a building's assessed value for tax purposes so the owner does not have to pay property tax on the increase in value resulting from the rehabilitation work.

In the case of a building worth $1 million before the work is done and $2 million after the rehabilitation work, with a J-51 exemption the building owner pays taxes only on the initial $1-million assessed value, less any abatement as described above. The law specifies certain classes of work that are eligible for J-51 benefits without making a distinction between exemptions and abatements.

For a building to receive an exemption, the rehabilitation work must have increased the assessed value of the property. Only major upgrades will have an appreciable effect on property values. Therefore, most rehabilitation work qualifies for J-51 abatements but not exemptions.

Read the RGB's rundown on J-51 exemptions and abatements online at http://www.housingnyc.com/html/resources/faq/421a-J51.html.

The appellate division of the New York Supreme Court ruled that the landlord for Stuyvesant Town and Peter Cooper Village, adjoining complexes with 11,232 apartments on the East Side of Manhattan, had improperly deregulated more than 3,000 apartments and raised rents beyond prescribed levels while receiving special property tax breaks from the city.

Tishman Speyer Properties could be liable for more than $200 million in fees if it is forced to repay tenants for improper rent increases for the four years prior to the lawsuit. Tenants facing rent increases of 20 to 30 percent filed a lawsuit in 2007 arguing that Tishman Speyer had no right to deregulate apartments in buildings that had received $24.5 million in tax breaks since 1992 under the J-51 program.

The results of this case are still playing out as of the writing of this book. Make sure you research any new changes to the laws when you begin buying.

At Your Service

Several New York firms specialize in shepherding landlords through the process of using investment incentives such as tax abatements and rebates. Building Equity is one of them. According to the company, current DHCR regulations allow investors to recoup the cost of qualifying major capital improvements (MCIs) over the course of seven years via rent increases.

That equates to a 14.29 percent return on investment once the increase has been approved. The addition of J-51 tax abatements can add further to this return. Building Equity works with clients to create an MCI strategy, execute the construction, and navigate the filing process.

Building Equity's premise is simple: through MCI-driven rent increases, apartment turnover is accelerated, thus creating additional financial gains. Furthermore, improvements such as new windows, boilers, and insulated roofs bring energy efficiency gains and increase the value of a building and the owner's bottom line.

There are obstacles to using J-51 credits, but the basic premise is straightforward and legal: you can buy a building, put on a new roof, and install a new boiler and pass the costs onto your rent-stabilized tenants. In its simplest form, this is just dollar-for-dollar on a risk-adjusted basis, which equates to the best returns available out there right now. The rents aren't going down because they are already priced below market value, and the buildings will remain occupied.

The low-income investment scenario doesn't come free of charge. Owners must be equipped to deal with landlord-tenant issues and a type of tenancy that's not easy to manage. The buildings themselves will be older and could need more repairs and maintenance than newer structures.

These factors don't always come together to create the perfect investment scenario, as owners in the Bronx found out a few decades ago. The 1970s were a tumultuous time in the Bronx. Hundreds of thousands of Jewish and Irish families were fleeing as this neighborhood deteriorated. Abandonment and arson were common. Tensions between landlords and tenants were explosively high.

The problem rolled into the 1980s, when the city was basically allowing people to buy buildings in these neighborhoods for $1, with the only requirement being that the new owner had to pay the back taxes and water charges that may have been on the building (sometimes those charges reached as high as $400,000 or $500,000). Investors could buy the building but had quite a mess to clean up in the wake of the previous owner's quick exodus.

The Bronx has since recovered from the mess and gone on to become a popular choice for investors looking for low-income-housing options. Still, it's important to know that success in that sector takes hard work and management finesse that the other two categories don't always require. Avoid overleveraging yourself and you should be able to follow in the footsteps of large institutional funds, all of which are prospering in the city's low-income market.

Luxury Accommodations

The last multifamily sector in New York City is the simplest to understand and navigate but is no less easy to execute. Unlike the two options already covered in this chapter, the luxury component doesn't involve rent stabilization and encompasses buildings that are entirely deregulated and feature new construction.

> **JUST THE FACTS**
>
> The term "new construction" in New York City includes structures that were built after 1974 and that are not subject to rent regulations.

In the luxury market, you won't be evicting tenants that have been paying low monthly rents for decades, nor will you find yourself thrown into landlord-tenant court over your intentions to raise rents by 2 percent. Typically, the luxury market comprises (on average) the highest-priced purchases in New York City. A 150-unit deregulated complex on the Upper East Side could conceivably sell for more than $500,000 to $600,000 per unit.

Institutional investors are drawn to the luxury space because it's a political "safety zone" for types that don't like to get involved with rent regulations. It's also easier to manage and mimics the "real-world" landlord-tenant relationships that you would find in other urban areas around the country. In essence, you own the building; the tenants don't own you.

There are also downsides to the luxury market. It's more susceptible to market swings. If you purchased a luxury building in Manhattan in mid-2008, for example, then your units' rents would have decreased anywhere from 5 to 25 percent as a result of faltering housing market conditions and a national recession. Rent and property value fluctuations can be positive or negative, depending on where you are in the economic cycle when you decide to buy the property.

Investors often buy luxury properties with the intention of converting them into condos or co-ops. Such buildings are easy to convert, but the process can be time-consuming and expensive. Expect to spend, at minimum, about $100,000 in legal, administrative, and filing fees. Conversions require the state attorney general's approval and typically take 12–18 months to finish.

The payoff can be significant. Take an apartment building that you are buying at X dollars per square foot. As a condo, the ultimate value may be three times that per-square-foot price if the market winds are at your back. You can typically generate a decent profit if you decide to convert to condo or co-op at the right time. At sales time just remember to consult a good tax advisor because the depending on how you structure your sales of units, your profit could be applied as ordinary income not capital gains.

> **Words to Know**
>
> **Condos:** Individual ownership of a portion of a building, with common areas shared by all owners. Maintenance fees called "assessments" are paid to the condominium association to maintain, repair, or improve the property.
>
> **Co-ops:** Similar to condominiums but without the exclusive ownership rights. Instead of owning the three-dimensional space and the interest in the "common elements" of the condo project, individuals own shares of a corporation that owns the entire project. They become "tenants" of this corporation with respect to the unit they occupy within the project.
>
> *continues* ▶

> **Condo conversion:** A conversion happens when a property of multiple living units goes from being held by one title owner to multiple title owners. Usually, the main purpose of such a transition is to take the property from being an income property to an owner-occupied residential dwelling.

The luxury market is fairly straightforward and includes buying options located in select "high-end" neighborhoods throughout the city. For the investor who has the resources to put into the market, the returns are both consistent and—particularly when strategies such as condo conversions are incorporated—impressive over time. The sector requires less confrontational management work than the low-income and owner-occupied approaches do, but the care of these assets cannot be taken for granted. High-end consumers in New York can be unforgiving.

Tying It All Together

Now you know about the three distinct categories of New York City's multifamily housing market and how they come together to make up the market as a whole. You've read examples of how owners have found success and faced challenges in their drive to maximize their investments. You'll be able to use this information as you compare opportunities, closed deals, and other aspects of the market in order to find the best possible choices for your situation.

In the next chapter, we'll look closely at various out-of-the-box deals that you should consider when investing in the city's multifamily market.

4
Out-of-the-Box

A person who speaks good English in New York sounds like a foreigner.

—Jackie Mason

There are a few unique deals that the New York City real estate market has to offer. You may be able to develop the empty space above your building (otherwise known as "air rights"), purchase developable land, or buy and rent out single-room-occupancy (SRO) units. All three of these options can be lucrative for investors who take the time to learn the ins and outs of such opportunities.

The fact that New York is a water-locked 24-hour city also creates an environment where out-of-the-box deals can work in an investor's favor. As we have said, unlike Los Angeles, where growth continues outward for two hours or more from the city's core, New York's geography is both limited and built out, and that transforms otherwise sleepy fringe real estate investments into unique local opportunities.

Air Rights

Air rights refer to the empty space above a property. They are a development right and one that the owner or renter of a piece of land or a building generally acquires when taking possession of the property.

> **DID YOU KNOW?**
>
> The legal concept of air rights is based on an ancient Latin saying: *Cuius est solum, eius est usque ad caelum et ad inferos* ("To whoever owns the land shall belong the earth, to its center and up to the heavens").

Air rights are a unique component of the NYC commercial market, where available land is scarce. In fact, the price of air rights has become a prominent measure within the market, where typical values are about 60 percent of comparable land values. Two primary factors determine the value of air rights: location and zoning. Popular neighborhoods tend to attract the most air rights transactions, as do those areas that are zoned with no building height limitations.

One of the most publicized air rights deals took place in New York City in 2005, when two developers agreed to pay a record price to build an apartment building with views of Central Park. Brothers William and Arthur Zeckendorf paid $430 a square foot (more than double the going rate of $200 per square foot) for the air rights over Park Avenue and East 60th Street. The deal allowed the Zeckendorfs to "build up" by developing a 35-story apartment tower that is taller than the zoning ordinarily allows.

> **DOING THE MATH**
>
> The height and size of any building in New York are determined by the floor-air ratio (FAR) of the zoning lot upon which it is being built. FAR is the ratio of the total floor area of buildings on a certain location to the size of the land of that location, or the limit imposed on such a ratio. To figure out the FAR, divide the total building square footage by the site size square footage.

Floor arearatio = total covered area on all floors of all buildings on a certain plot divided by the area of the plot

A FAR of 2.0, for example, would mean that the total floor area of a building is two times the gross area of the plot on which it is constructed (as in the case of a multistory structure).

To find out the cost per buildable square foot, take the lot size, multiply it by the FAR, and divide that into the cost of the land. Use the real estate calculator at http://reicalc.com/reim/calculators/FAR.cfm. Plug in your numbers and come up with the total buildable square footage for a specific piece of property.

Investors looking to maximize air rights must know the zoning laws in their targeted area(s). Two of the best resources for this type of information are the New York City Department of Planning (http://www.nyc.gov/html/dcp/html/lucds/cdstart.shtml) and the New York City Zoning Handbook (http://www.tenant.net/Other_Laws/zoning/zonch03.html), both of which contain vital information on the city's zoning laws.

You Never Know Whats Going to Pop Up

My partner Joe and I were recently called out to a property by an owner who wanted to sell his 9th Avenue building. Aptly named Peep World, the business catered to the adult crowd. It wasn't generating much revenue, but it was in a great location that included thousands of square feet in air rights that made the underlying real estate worth more than the building itself.

So there we were on the third floor of the building at 9 a.m., discussing the sale with the owner, when a few grubby cab drivers come sauntering in, pull the curtains on the Peep World rooms, and insert their quarters into the box. Seconds later we were listening to really bad porn from behind the curtains and the accompanying grunts and groans that go along with the package. For sure this added an interesting element to the meeting. My partner and I couldn't keep straight faces. The owner went on as if we were sitting in a quiet conference room. I guess you get used to that stuff when you own the joint . . . as they say "only in New York."

continues ▶

> The not so funny part is that the real "oohs" and "aahs" came when he sold that building for almost $10 million because of the value of his air rights. Furthermore, that contract was then sold or "flipped" to a buyer who ultimately paid $11 million to close on the property.

New York City's 59 community districts, established by local law in 1975, illustrate the diversity of the city's land uses and population. They range in size from fewer than 900 acres to almost 15,000 and in population from fewer than 35,000 residents to more than 200,000.

In New York, residence districts are designated by the prefix "R" in the Zoning Resolution. There are 10 standard residence districts in New York City, R1 through R10. The numbers refer to the permitted density (R1 having the lowest density, R10 the highest) and certain other controls such as required parking. A second letter or number signifies additional controls in certain districts. Unless otherwise stated, the regulations for each of the 10 residence districts pertain to all subcategories within that district. The R4 district, for example, encompasses R4-1, R4A, and R4B.

Within the city's standard districts, R1 and R2 allow only detached single-family residences and certain community facilities. The R3-2 through R10 districts accept all types of dwelling units and community facilities and are distinguished by differing bulk and density, height and setback, parking, and lot coverage or open-space requirements.

Did You Know?

You don't have to give up your air rights when you sell a piece of property. Simply sell the building but retain the air rights to sell at a later date. Make sure a knowledgeable attorney advises you on the structure of this type of a transaction.

It's also important to note that R3-2 districts permit detached and semidetached houses, garden apartments, rowhouse developments, and a broader range of community facilities. R4 and RS zones are primarily districts of rowhouses and small multiple dwellings. The R6 through R9 districts without a letter suffix (R8 rather than R8A, for example) encourage on-site open space and on-site parking.

> ### Air Rights in Action
>
> In 2007, an entity controlled by Argent Ventures bought the land under Grand Central Terminal and all its unused air rights.
>
> The deal, which is known as Midtown Trackage, also gave Argent all the property under, along, and over a total of 156 miles of railroad tracks that run through Manhattan, the Bronx, and Westchester, Putnam, and Dutchess counties.
>
> The price was about $80 million for the unused rights, which could at some point translate into the development of apartments, retail, and office buildings.

One of the more controversial air rights acquisitions in New York City involved none other than Donald Trump, whose Turtle Bay construction project was called Trump World Tower. Stretching 39 stories into the sky, the same number of floors as the UN headquarters across the street, the building came about after Trump quietly purchased air rights sufficient to build his tower 70 stories tall. Reaching 861 feet into the air, it was the tallest residential building in the world from 2000 to 2002, when it was surpassed by Tower Palace Three in Seoul.

Before this transaction, an investor could purchase air rights from any building on the block and transfer them to his or her own lot, allowing the construction of an extremely tall building. Now, thanks to the Trump deal, one can use air rights only from an adjacent property—thus severely limiting an owner's ability to amass those rights.

Even with the new rules, expect to see more "air-oriented" deals surface in the future in New York City, where land is scarce and demand for it is high. Those owners that don't place a value on the available air—and who don't realize that the addition of a penthouse unit can add significant value to a building—are missing out on a lucrative aspect of the city's real estate market.

Developable Land

New York City's population continues to grow despite the fact that everyone is situated on a tiny island with limited developable land. When this book went to press, rental vacancy rates were at a high point, as a result of the economic downturn that began in 2007, of about 4.5 percent—a number that would be unheard of in most American metropolitan areas.

When an investor can get his or her hands on developable land, it can be a lot like hitting a gold mine. While scarce, there are select opportunities available to the investor who has the financial resources to put into developable land. Such opportunities come with an expensive price tag but can be extremely profitable over time.

However, the purchase of developable land in New York City is also the most risky investment out there. The most successful investors in this category avoid leveraging themselves when closing the deal, and they realize that their investments are highly illiquid and subject to megatrends in value.

In the secondary markets, when real estate values are on the rise, developable land can be flipped for a quick profit—but don't count on this strategy. You don't want to be the last one standing when values decline and demand wanes.

> **LESSONS LEARNED**
>
> Consider the scene in Miami in the early 2000s, when investors got caught up in a land grab and an overbuilding of the area's condo market. At one point, the city of about 400,000 people had more than 60,000 condo units at some stage of planning, permitting, or construction.
>
> A few years later, many who were hoping to flip the land for a profit have been left holding the bag. The market tumbled, condo buyers retreated, and the foreclosure signs started going up all over the place. Overconstruction of condominium units has been widely blamed for a severe downturn in the Miami real estate market following a boom from 2000 to 2005.
>
> When this book went to press, Miami's historically overbuilt condo market had imploded, with more than 25,000 units languishing and owners growing increasingly frantic to unload them.
>
> This is just one example of the risk involved with acquiring developable land in New York City or anywhere else in the nation. To play successfully in this category, you have to know what you're doing, or you need an endless cash supply to cushion your portfolio from any fluctuations.

If you are going to buy a piece of land for $1 million and take out a $500,000 loan on it, make sure you have a plan in place. (One of my current clients purchased a $50-million piece of land on Madison Avenue in Midtown and wasn't able to start construction quickly enough. Now it's costing him more than $1 million a quarter in loan payments.) Line up the right financial partners and be ready to withstand time and construction delays or you'll quickly find yourself underwater in this risky investment field. If you use leverage, purchasing land is the most risky investment one can make.

That said, they're not making any more of it in New York, so in this market it is most likely more secure than any other market in the country,. We all know the most famous boom-bust land locations: Florida, California, and Texas.

Single-Room Occupancy (SRO)

This is one of my favorite types of buildings in the city. A single-room occupancy (more commonly SRO, sometimes called single-resident occupancy) refers to a multiple-tenant building that houses one or two people in individual rooms (sometimes two rooms or two rooms with a bathroom or half-bathroom) or to the single-room dwelling itself. Simply put, it's just a box with a sink.

SRO tenants typically share bathrooms and kitchens. Although some SRO rooms may include kitchenettes, bathrooms, or half-baths, most do not. Many are former hotels, and SROs are primarily rented as residences to a range of people from travelers, students, lowlifes, and drifters to just about anyone. Many units in SROs used to be rented nightly and were a haven for drugs, crime, prostitution, and the like. You will know you are in an SRO when you recognize that particular smell. It is hard to describe, but it is a little like stale piss mixed with alcohol.

> ### Did You Know?
> The term "SRO" originated in New York City in the 1930s, but the nickname is thought to date back at least 50 years prior.

In the late 1970s and early 1980s, with the help of significant government subsidies, developers bought an estimated 100,000 of the city's 200,000 SRO rooms and converted them into offices, co-ops, and condominiums. Between 1970 and 1983, according to the Community Service Society, a nonprofit organization serving the poor, 87 percent of the city's SRO rooms disappeared, with many potential renters winding up homeless.

In 1993, there were 44,000 SRO rooms left in New York, according to a survey conducted by the Department of Housing Preservation and Development. Now, the remainder are being converted as the city experiences its second wave of conversions, which began in the late 1990s. One indicator of the trend is the increase in requests for "certificates of no harassment," which the department requires of owners who want to convert SROs. In the most recent year, such requests covered 1,683 rooms in Manhattan, about the same as the year before.

According to the New York City Department of Housing Preservation and Development, each SRO room has a maximum occupancy of two adults, no residents may be younger than 16 years old, and each sleeping room must have at least one window that faces outside. Building managers of SROs are required to reside in the building. The NY State Division of Housing and Community Renewal (DHCR) regulates rents for most SRO buildings.

SRO building owners who wish to alter the number of rooms, transform rooms into apartments, or change the number of kitchen and bathroom facilities must first receive a certificate of no harassment (CNH) from the Department of Housing Preservation and Development (HPD). While the requirement is designed to protect the rights of SRO residents, many owners complain that the process is marred by incompetent people and bureaucratic hurdles.

As the owner, you have to fill out a lengthy questionnaire with all the current and former residents' names and known addresses (even if the house is empty). Then, HPD is supposed to make an effort to contact all these people to make sure they weren't forced out against their will. In one owner's case, after this mail campaign came up clean, he was told over the phone that everything was fine and to expect the CNH within the week.

"When we called back three weeks later, we found out that HPD had decided to send someone out on foot to try to talk to all the former tenants, thus adding another month to the timeline. At some point in the process, an HPD inspector has to come inspect your house to make sure there are no signs of tenants still living there; at the time, there was only one inspector for the five boroughs," the SRO owner states. "The entire process took about four months, even with the benefit of a friend in city government periodically lobbing in calls to HPD on our behalf."

One SRO Owner's Rant

The owner of an SRO building discussed his recent CNH application and the entire process on his blog (http://www.brownstoner.com/renovations/2005/02/the_landmarks_p.html):

> "We had a huge breakthrough this week: After almost seven friggin' months we finally got our Certificate of Non Harassment from the Department of Housing Preservation and Development (HPD). What a joke the whole process is—riddled with human incompetence and bureaucratic strangles. We understand why the process exists—to protect the rights of poor tenants—but we think the system needs a major overhaul.
>
> "We have heard of people buying empty shells that were formerly SRO's who end up spending countless months wading through the paperwork. In our case, most of the former tenants were drug dealers (one of whom held up our neighbor at gun point a couple of years ago). Given that there are well over a hundred case files in the pipeline at any time, the Department is woefully understaffed: There is one inspector for all five boroughs and one person responsible for managing the paper work flow. If they are going to keep this system in place—and we've heard rumors that a revamping is in the works—they should increase the application fee from $150 and hire some more people. Someone who's bought a $1 million home and is burning up $5,000 a month in carrying costs would be willing to pay a significant amount of money to expedite the process."

SROs are a good out-of-the-box choice for investors who are willing to put the time into learning the ins and outs of this type of real estate. SRO establishments have long occupied the bottom end of New York's lodging food chain, where travelers and those who can't afford traditional apartments or homes rent rooms by the week or month.

The better SROs in New York serve as inexpensive housing for the old or ill or for those who have fallen out of the middle class and are struggling to keep themselves afloat. In each, there is typically a mix of drug addicts, AIDS sufferers, the recently homeless, and/or a combination of all three.

There's a need for SROs in New York's housing market and an opportunity for investors to put their money into this type of housing. Such buildings are subject to some regulations to which other residential structures are not. For example, SRO buildings must provide one toilet, one washbasin, and one bath or shower for every six SRO units. In addition, every floor where tenants reside must have bathroom facilities.

In addition to the CNH requirement, there are other challenges to consider before investing in SRO property. On the financial side, the risks associated with renting out units for as little as $150 a month are high. If the tenants don't pay, it can cost you more to collect a single month's rent than you could receive in one year of renting out the SRO unit.

SRO owners should also prepare themselves for surprises that many landlords don't have to contend with. I know a landlord who bought an SRO building and a few days later decided to upgrade its electrical system. He opened small patches in the walls throughout the building, not knowing that the tenants would turn the orifices into convenient stashing places for their drugs and other illegal goodies. He figured it out after getting a few frantic calls from tenants who complained that a junkie was freaking out in the hallway and scratching at the walls because his "stash" had been plastered over. I guess this is partly why I like this product type so much. It happens to attract ownership scenarios that most good fiction writers would have a hard time competing with. Again, only in New York.

SRO Web Sites

Frequently Asked Questions for Residential Building Owners
http://www.nyc.gov/html/hpd/html/owners/faqs-for-res-owners.shtml

Goddard Riverside Community Center (works in favor of SRO tenants, watch out for them)
http://www.goddard.org/srolawproject.html

SROs are highly restrictive, with strict rules regarding when and by how much rents can be increased—typically by much lower percentages than traditional apartments. See chapters 1 and 2 for more information on how the rents are set and how much they can be increased annually.

Investors who want to maximize their SRO investments have three options: convert the building into a short-term hotel/youth hostel; triple-net-lease it out to an organization, nonprofit, school, or other institution that will "overrent" it from you (based on the building's high-density housing status); or, because these buildings typically are in disrepair and contain many rent-stabilized tenants, vacate the building and convert it to another use. The latter can be extremely profitable but may require a lot of paperwork and time to complete.

The SRO market is the most management intensive and requires the most attention to detail. It can also be a stable, lucrative investment choice for people who are willing to get face to face with tenants, be physically present at their buildings, and take the time to understand the market.

The Final Word

The New York market offers unique opportunities for investors who want to break out of the traditional real estate molds. Air rights give owners an advantage in terms of both property value and potential. Developable land provides a risky yet profitable way to acquire property in the city. SROs are a good choice for those looking for a steady, predictable income and who aren't afraid to roll up their sleeves and take a hands-on approach to landlording.

With all three deal types, investors looking to change the use of their properties wind up with even bigger returns. Depending on the current economic conditions, the owner who transitions between these three types of real estate can reap significant rewards. By understanding the various uses and possibilities of the pieces of real estate that they're playing with in New York, investors can open up a whole new world for themselves.

For example, one investor might seek out a property that has a lot of air rights associated with it, with the intention of someday tapping those rights to enhance the value of the property. Another individual might want to purchase a multistory building where a handful of SRO tenants reside, knowing that he or she will be able to create value out of those rooms in the future.

Investors who explore and learn about out-of-the-box deals hold a distinct advantage over those who do not. It's just too much work for the typical investor who isn't willing to put in the time and energy to understanding the associated legal and material concepts (such as the architectural and engineering aspects of the project).

Few have expended the energy necessary to win in this aspect of the New York City real estate game. Investors who do cross over that line from real estate and into the legal, zoning, usage, architectural, and engineering concepts involved with such projects are the ones who realize the bigger profits.

5
Debt and Equity

Money is better than poverty, if only for financial reasons.

—WOODY ALLEN

You can't get into any market—never mind the New York City real estate market—without a working knowledge of the roles that debt and equity play in putting together an investment deal. In this chapter, we'll look at the basics of debt and equity in the city's real estate market and show you the best strategies for financing a deal, negotiating that financing, selecting a form of equity, and forming a successful real estate syndicate.

Debt

There are several ways that you can finance a real estate deal in New York. The first is to use your own cash and/or resources to create a situation where your property isn't leveraged at all and you own it outright. Many "old-time" New York families purchased real estate this way and still do.

The younger generations are anathema to that strategy. Because buying "all cash" isn't feasible for many, the next-best options are to get financing from local banks and government-backed lenders and loans from banks who then resell those loans in the form of commercial-backed securities (CMBS), a market that all but shut down in 2008 as a result of the credit crisis and recession that gripped the country. That has left a huge gap in financing sources for many real estate investors. For reference, in 2007, there was more than $200 billion in CMBS loans originated for commercial real estate transactions. Here's a look at each option:

Local Banks

In New York, institutions such as Astoria Federal, Dime Savings Bank, New York Community Bank, and Intervest National Bank regularly lend money to real estate investors. These banks make the loans and keep them on their own balance sheets instead of "selling" them to other entities. Decisions are made at the local level rather than having to confer with out-of-state headquarters, and investors have the chance to form long-term relationships with their local bankers.

Local banks are the most popular choice for investors in New York City. Your bank needs to understand the rent-stabilized marketplace, and what better place to go than local? They give the buyer the most credit in terms of dollars and sense, and because they don't sell off loans, their lending products typically maintain the interest rates that were negotiated at the outset.

> **DID YOU KNOW?**
>
> There are three types of banks: nationwide, regional, and local. Here's a rundown of each:
>
> **Nationwide banks** offer several lending products to real estate investors. These large institutions provide consumer and commercial mortgage businesses with several options. On the downside, they offer little or no flexibility for the short-term real estate investor. However, as your business is established, they can serve as a secure business line of credit for future projects.
>
> **Regional banks** are smaller and usually comprise several branches spread across one or more states. Like local banks, they are portfolio lenders that hold the loans "in house," unlike nationwide lenders that sell the loans to a secondary lender. This gives smaller banks the most flexibility to set terms and guidelines.

Local banks are similar to regional banks but normally have even fewer branches. They are also portfolio lenders, and they typically offer the most flexibility and customer service when working with investors.

Local banks will determine whether to loan money after they assess your financial situation, the deal itself, and your management experience. You will have to fill out a loan application and provide tax returns and information about the asset you are purchasing so the bank's underwriters can "size the loan." Expect the process to take 30 to 90 days, particularly for first-time borrowers.

To find the right bank, consider which institutions offer the type of loan that you're seeking. Talk to attorneys, accountants, and real estate professionals about their experiences in working with local banks, and select one that is best suited for your particular transaction.

Government-Backed Financing

Your next financing option is government-backed financing, which is lent by Freddie Mac, Fannie Mae, and FHA/HUD.

> **KEY DEFINITIONS**
>
> **Conforming loan:** A loan that has underwriting criteria consistent with the strict guidelines of Fannie Mae, Freddie Mac, FHA, or VA. These are typically the lowest-interest-rate loans, with very good terms.
>
> **Fannie Mae (FNMA):** Federal National Mortgage Association, a federally chartered corporation that purchases mortgages and packages them to sell as securities.
>
> **Freddie Mac (FHMLC):** Federal Home Loan Mortgage Corporation, a federally chartered corporation that purchases mortgages and packages them to sell as securities.
>
> *continues* ▶

> **FHA loans:** The Federal Housing Administration (FHA), which is part of the U.S. Department of Housing and Urban Development (HUD), administers various mortgage loan programs. FHA loans have lower down payment requirements and are easier to qualify for than conventional loans.

These three entities offer government-insured mortgages that usually take a lot longer to close than bank loans, but they feature the best interest rates available on the market.

Government-backed funding equates to more money at a cheaper rate, but you will pay for it in other ways that may not be attractive to some investors. There's a lot of paperwork to complete; the bank underwriters will do extensive and, by some opinions, unnecessary analysis; and the operational regulations one has to follow when borrowing through Freddie Mac, Fannie Mae, or FHA/HUD can be limiting. For example, they will likely impose restrictions on investors who want to complete rehabilitations on the property in question. You have to follow their guidelines or you won't get funded.

Whether you decide to use government-backed financing will depend on your options and potentially lack thereof. If you are an investor who likes to be in control and make all the decisions, then you may not have the patience to deal with this funding source. The one good thing about buying in New York City is there always seems to be a source of financing somewhere and often at rates and terms competitive to those offered by the government-backed mortgages.

Securitized Lending

Loans are available from many of the Wall Street banks through a lending program called commercial mortgage-backed securities, or CMBS. Investors work with banks that make several different loans and then package those loans together and "sell" the loan payments as bonds to investors. Those bonds are backed by the cash flow from the batch of commercial mortgages that the bank made.

This type of loan ultimately places your mortgage into a trust with other real estate loans, and then that trust is sold as bonds to investors. A bank may issue money on several mortgages on commercial properties and then collateralize that cash flow from the mortgages into bonds. Those bonds are then sold to institutions.

Here's an example of how the CMBS market works:

> A bank issues $200 million in mortgages at an average rate of 6 percent. The institution then sells bonds against this collateralized cash flow for 5 percent and collects a 1 percent spread.
>
> The bank makes money on the spread, and the bond buyers have less risk because their cash flow is not tied to one property but is diversified across a number of properties. The higher the rating on the bond, the less risk associated with the cash flow.

By taking out a CMBS loan on your investment property, you can obtain a larger mortgage loan (more dollars) and usually a lower-interest cost. Because the mortgage liability isn't held by the bank itself, the institution can lend more money to potential borrowers. Banks win because they can make more loans by pooling the loans together and selling them off as bundles.

Calling the Shots

If you've been alive the past few years, you've seen the news: all of the investment banks have gotten into trouble—some of them as a result of the securitized lending environment.

You have to realize that when you have a commercial loan with a traditional bank, it's easy to draw conclusions about what's driving each of the elements (including the bank, the property, the loan, and the borrower). When you use a CMBS loan, a fifth element comes into play: the bond investors. What drives these investors is often not related to what's happening at your property but what is going on in the financial industry.

You need to know who is calling the shots; it's usually the people with the money. Within the CMBS market, those people ultimately are the bond investors, who are concerned with many other things besides your property. As of the writing of this book, it remains to be seen how the financing issues for the CMBS market will be resolved, and for sure, it will be something for the history books.

With this type of financing, it's important to understand that adding your property to the CMBS "pool" means that you're locking it into a bundle. Taking it out of that bundle (to sell it, for example) could result in penalties. Be sure to check with your lender about these and other restrictions before taking out a CMBS loan.

Negotiating Financing

The amount of cash flow a new owner realizes from a property is often established during the acquisition phase and based on the financing structure. The most successful real estate investors rely on sharp negotiation skills to get the terms they want on a deal. Going beyond price, there are also down payments, taking back seconds, taking over existing debt and mortgages, short-term and long-term owner financing, conditional clauses, and a long list of other factors that can be negotiated.

> ### Top Negotiating Tips
>
> - Ask. Negotiators often fail to raise an issue because they don't think they have a chance of success.
> - Never negotiate against yourself. Once you make an offer, wait for a response before making another offer.
> - Get it in writing. When parties fail to live up to an agreement, written proof of the negotiators' intent is critical.
> - Prepare. Learn as much as possible about the needs and wants of your side and the needs and wants of the other side.
> - Know your bottom line. If you know what you want beforehand, you'll know when it's time to stop.
> - Establish a plan B. Know your best alternative if you face an unsuccessful negotiation.
> - Listen to the other side. Good negotiators are good listeners and good communicators, not just good talkers.
> - Don't be afraid of confrontation. Negotiations should not be arguments, but avoiding tough issues is not productive.
> - Make sure you are working with a broker who is providing you the best possible information.

To ensure success during this stage, be sure to come to the table thoroughly prepared and armed with the research that you need to make your points. Avoid making quick decisions, and instead rely on your due diligence and cool head to help you through the negotiation period. Think everything over carefully, and don't overlook these important points that can affect an investor's cash flow:

Points, service, and other charges
Most banks will charge 1 percent to fund a loan, along with the costs of all third-party reports (appraisal, environmental, and engineering) and legal fees. Most mortgage brokers will charge 1 percent as well. In an environment where interest rates are bouncing wildly, look to "lock" your interest rate until the transaction closes, buffeting yourself from interest rate risk. Finally, in NYC there is a mortgage-recording tax that is approximately 3 percent of the loan amount. When added all up, there are significant closing costs on the purchasing end of NYC real estate. Be prepared.

Additional funding
If you're going to make improvements to the property that would increase rentals during the short period following the initial funding date, negotiate a loan provision for additional advances that will increase the loan amount under those conditions.

Release clauses
A release clause is a provision in a mortgage that allows for the freeing of part of a property (such as when the property being purchased is under construction or renovation) from the mortgage after a proportional amount of the mortgage has been paid.

Annual financial reports
Audited financial reports are expensive, but many lenders require them at the end of each fiscal year. When negotiating, see whether the institution will take a compilation statement prepared by an independent CPA instead.

Appraisals
The lender typically selects the appraiser, but if you have an appraisal that's already been prepared by a qualified professional, see whether the lender will use it instead. Not only will it be cheaper for you but also using the existing appraisal will expedite the lending process.

LATE CHARGES

Include a provision that late charges will not be effective until a specified period from the due date.

Equity

Technically defined as the difference between the market value of a property and the claims held against it, or otherwise known as "the cash you have to put in," equity is the most important consideration for real estate investors. It's particularly important for New York City investors, who have the tendency to buy properties and hold them for a very long time. For this long-term approach to work, all equity partners must be on the same page from the outset, with everyone investing and operating in the same rhythm.

> **SIMPLE WISDOM**
>
> Ofer Yardeni was born in Israel in 1960 and immigrated to the United States in 1986. He launched his career as a real estate salesperson and today is managing partner and cofounder of Stonehenge Partners, a New York City–based real estate owner and operator that owns and manages a 3-million-square-foot portfolio valued at approximately $2 billion.
>
> Yardeni once told me about the Hebrew parable of not harvesting fruit off of a tree for seven years, as the plant matures. There's a lot of simple wisdom in this theory that can be applied in real estate. You have to allow the investment to mature before expecting to pull money out of it, à la "Sell the milk, not the cow."

Without this cohesiveness, your real estate investment plan may involve more brain damage than you are signing up for in the beginning. As you will find when you look around this business, many people enter the real estate world because they think it is an easy way to make money. Not the case. When you are successful, the money comes easily; becoming successful is not easy.

Selecting the Form of Entity

A real estate syndicate involves two or more people or entities that join together to finance the purchase and sale of real estate properties, typically those requiring significant capital.

However, a syndicate is not an actual form of ownership. Instead, the investors involved must decide what legal form to use to hold the real estate. For example, the syndicate might be organized as a corporation, general or limited partnership, joint venture, or limited-liability company (LLC). The corresponding responsibilities, obligations, and relationships between the investors are determined mainly by the form in which the syndicate is organized. Here are your choices:

> **Did You Know?**
>
> The popularity of real estate syndications has grown over the years, in response to vibrant real estate markets throughout the country. There are various laws and regulations that govern the actual formation and day-to-day operations of real estate syndications. These laws will vary by state, and it is important that you speak with a qualified real estate attorney in New York City for more information.

Corporations

A corporation is a legal entity that is created under state law. A corporation's charter, sometimes called its articles of incorporation, sets forth the powers of the corporation, including its ability to buy real estate. While some corporate charters permit the purchase of real estate for any reason, others limit it to buying land necessary to fulfill the entity's corporate purposes.

One of the main advantages of the corporate form of ownership is that its shareholders enjoy limited liability. This means that if the business were to incur significant debts, only the business itself would be liable. The shareholders' investment in the corporation is limited to their investment in company stock, and they are not responsible for any company losses.

The biggest disadvantage is that corporations are subject to double taxation. A corporation must file an income tax return and pay tax on its profits. Then, when a corporation distributes dividends to shareholders, it must pay tax on the dividends at its own personal income tax rate.

S Corporations

To avoid double taxation, many real estate investors use a modified corporate form known as the S corporation. This alternate form of ownership allows limited shareholder liability but eliminates double taxation. An S corporation allows the syndicate to pass income through without taxation at the corporate level. Shareholders pay tax on distributions only at their personal income tax rate. S corporations are limited to smaller businesses because a maximum of 75 shareholders is permitted.

In addition, the corporation must elect to be treated as an S corporation. Failure to do so or to comply with other requirements governing their structure and operation will result in the loss of the favored tax status. S corporations typically are used for somewhat smaller real estate transactions.

Real Estate Partnerships

Real estate partnerships have long been used to acquire, operate, and hold real estate. A partnership is an association composed of two or more individuals to operate a business for profit as co-owners. By pooling their resources, partners have greater leverage in buying property and can combine their skills in managing the property. Here are the different types of partnerships:

- **General partnership:** All of the partners actively participate in the management and day-to-day business operations. Any business losses are shared among the partners, who are fully liable for all partnership debts. To mitigate this risk, a partnership typically will purchase insurance. However, if one partner dies, withdraws from the partnership, or files for bankruptcy, the partnership automatically terminates. To continue operations, the remaining partners must enter into a new partnership agreement.
- **Limited partnership:** This type of partnership consists of one or more limited and general partners. The limited partners typically provide capital and arrange the financing but do not take an active role in running the business. The limited partners receive a share of the profits for their role as limited partners but are not liable for the business's debts. Instead, their liability is limited to their capital contribution. However, if limited partners begin actively taking part in the control of the business, they will lose their limited liability.

Did You Know?

Many states (including New York) have adopted the Revised Uniform Limited Partnership Act (RULPA), which expressly authorizes limited partnerships to own real estate and recognizes the limited liability of limited partners. It also provides that profits and losses are to be passed through the partnership to the partners, who are taxed on any profits at their own personal income tax rate.

RULPA also lists certain actions that limited partners can take without losing their limited-liability status. For example, a limited partner may vote on whether:

- a general partner should be admitted or removed.
- the nature of the business should be changed.
- the business should be dissolved.
- assets of the limited partnership should be sold, leased, mortgaged, or otherwise transferred.
- the limited partnership should incur debt other than in the ordinary course of business.

- **Joint venture:** This is a partnership in which two or more individuals join together to conduct a specific business enterprise. While a joint venture must be created by agreement between the parties to share in the venture's losses and profits, it is created for one specific project rather than to carry on a continuing business relationship.

    Most partnerships carry out a general business purpose over a period of years, and the death of a joint venture member does not automatically dissolve the joint venture. Another difference is that a participant in a joint venture does not have the power to bind the others, whereas partners may agree that each has full power to bind the partnership.

- **Limited-liability companies:** An LLC is a hybrid entity, combining the most attractive features of limited partnerships and corporations. Like a corporation, LLC members are protected from individual liability for the LLC's debts and losses. However, an LLC need not comply with the formalities of corporate minutes, bylaws, directors, and shareholders but has a more flexible management structure. For tax purposes, the LLC itself pays no income tax. Like a partnership, all of the income and losses flow through directly to the members, who must report such items on their individual income tax returns.

It's important to understand the different forms of ownership before selecting the right one for your real estate investment plan. Some types give owners absolute ownership of the property for unlimited duration, while others give ownership only during an individual's life. Review all of the options before making a decision, and be sure to factor in the legal, financial, and tax considerations when making your selection.

Types of Equity

Your business partners can include wealthy individuals, private equity funds, hedge funds, opportunity funds, or any other entity that has money to invest and agrees with your real estate investment approach.

Raising private money from wealthy individuals allows you to source funds from any successful people in industry. These potential equity partners are prevalent in New York City, and most of them are continually on the lookout for profitable places to invest their money.

FOREIGN MONEY

Foreign investors from all over the world are interested in New York City, with the major draws being appreciation, stability, capital appreciation, and other debt and equity advantages that don't exist outside of the United States. New York City consistently ranks as a top spot for foreign real estate investment, according to the Association of Foreign Investors in Real Estate annual survey.

For example, Russian millionaires love the U.S. property market and are lured by distressed sales and the ruble's rise against the dollar, according to New York City lawyer Edward Mermelstein, who has closed hundreds of real estate deals for buyers from the former Soviet Union since 2007.

One New York City broker recently signed contracts with a group of foreign nationals from Spain, Italy, and Columbia for 32 apartments in one building for about $41 million. Another broker says foreign investors are taking advantage of the lower dollar and motivated U.S. sellers, following a trend of an increase of acquisitions by foreigners of all nationalities who see a benefit in owning freehold properties in the New York market and the diversification of their investments portfolios.

Recently, an Abu Dhabi sovereign wealth fund bought a controlling stake in the Chrysler Building, a fixture of the Manhattan skyline that was the world's tallest building until 1933. The purchase was the second acquisition of a New York landmark by a Middle Eastern fund within a month's time.

Expect the trend to grow. As you get more sophisticated in looking for equity, you shouldn't turn down the possibility of raising money from overseas.

New York is also replete with private equity, hedge, and opportunity funds that invest in the commercial real estate market. With so many large funds based in New York City, the finance center of the United States, organizations such as Gramercy Capital and Colony Capital are continually raising money that gets invested back into the region's real estate market.

Bargain Shopping

With plans to raise $600 million in a public offering of shares in its commercial property investment fund, New York–based Apollo Global Management LLC is gearing up to buy properties in major cities through its REIT, Apollo Commercial Real Estate Finance Inc. The fund is also looking to buy commercial mortgage-backed securities.

Apollo seeks to buy real estate from commercial property owners that are unable to refinance an estimated $1.2 trillion of loans expected to mature in the next three years.

Many of these funds look at real estate as a fourth asset class, with the investment option becoming more mainstream for funds that traditionally put their money in stocks and bonds. Fortress Investment Group, for example, recently purchased a $640-million Manhattan condominium known as Scheffield, a project being built by New York developer Kent Swig, through a foreclosure proceeding.

Raising money from private equity funds and similar entities can be tricky and usually requires a track record. You have to look and *be* the part. The difference is that instead of raising $100,000 from 20 different wealthy individuals to get $2 million in equity, you need only endorse a single $2-million check when you're working with a sole partner. The paperwork and logistics are easier, yet getting that one entity to buy into your plan could be more difficult.

The recent economic and market turmoil hasn't made the situation any easier for real estate investors. In the high times of the 2000s, many of these funds were making decisions by simply allocating "$10 million here" and another "$20 million there," more casually than other times in financial history. Today, they're operating in an uncertain real estate market, decisions are requiring more diligence, and risky propositions are not finding an audience. Still, the opportunity exists to work with these funds, particularly if your real estate investment approach is airtight and you have the experience to back it up.

Managing Real Estate Investments

Real estate syndication requires management strategies (aka your internal "investor relations department"), including communication with investors, handling of relations between the investors and the syndicator, and management of the legal entity itself. (This is distinguished from supervision and operation of the property itself, which is known as property management. See chapter 7 of this book for more information on property management.) This section discusses some of the important management considerations associated with real estate syndication.

Reports and Distributions

Distributing reports on the operation of a property on a regular basis to investors is a good way to build rapport between the syndicator and the investors. The reports should include enough detail to help the investor develop a clear picture of the property's current operating success. The reporting process should also include the mailing of an annual financial statement, the entity tax return or partners' K1s, and a summary of the year's operating history.

Whether you hold annual meetings is a personal decision. While formal meetings can help establish rapport and create a professional image for the syndicate and its investments, they can also be expensive and time-consuming. Another option is simply to host an annual party or gathering where investors have the opportunity to meet you and ask questions.

Building Your Team

Before you start investing in the New York City real estate market, you'll want to assemble a competent team of experts who can advise you on how make the best possible financial decisions. Here are the two most important professionals you'll want to have on your team:

Accountants

Some 55 percent of Americans rely on professionals to file their tax returns. That need becomes even greater when you establish a business that requires tax advice. As you begin your research into various types of property you might buy, do not forget to ask professionals, property owners, and other people in the know whether there are good accountants in the area. You can start your search the following ways:

- Talk to friends, family members, and coworkers or your state's CPA society for referrals.
- Talk to local real estate agents or brokers for referrals.
- Call a local real estate association for referrals.
- Prepare a list of questions pertaining to your situation. Most accountants will answer simple questions over the phone at no charge.
- Ask how much each accountant charges per hour and request an estimate of the time needed to complete the tasks you require.

The most important assistance tax professionals can provide for your real estate activities involves helping you plan the life cycle of that investment. This will allow you to focus on your goals and avoid overpaying taxes when you renovate, buy more property, or close out your holdings. Your accountant, in conjunction with your attorney, can also help you decide whether you need to make the transition to a formal business structure to accomplish these goals.

Attorneys

When you are buying and selling or owning and managing investment property, you are running a business, and you need to handle business matters professionally. With the complexity of ever-changing regulations and tenant and tax laws affecting real estate today, you may need an attorney to keep abreast of the rules. In the end, an attorney's guidance may save you far more than his or her fees.

Be sure to consult an attorney before you get into any investment. Secure an hour or two of a professional's time to discuss planning all aspects of the transaction. This initial, exploratory conversation with an attorney, a tax advisor, or both can shape your view of what you are buying, when and where you buy it, or whether you should be buying it at all.

Following the Rules

Regardless of which entity you choose or who is involved with it, your real estate syndicate will be subject to both state and federal regulation. Because syndicates fall under securities law and because most states have laws regulating the sale of securities, you'll want to either do your own homework or work with an attorney who is experienced in this arena to figure out exactly what rules need to be followed.

New York State has a "blue sky law" (otherwise known as the Martin Act) that regulates the sale of securities. The law requires the registration of all securities offerings and sales, as well as of stockbrokers and brokerage firms. Administered by the state's regulatory agency, the laws provide private causes of action for private investors who have been injured by securities fraud. Investors in real estate syndicates must comply with the law.

Brokerage commissions and finders' fees also fall under the regulatory umbrella because a license is required to engage in activities connected with the offering and sale of any interest in a real estate syndicate. New York's real estate syndication rules are not as strict as in some states (which require the property managers to be licensed, for example) but still need to be studied and heeded to avoid unnecessary penalties, fines, and other problems.

6

The Role of the Architect in Real Estate Investing

Frank Gehry. Antoni Gaudi. Frank Lloyd Wright. Architects do not just change the landscapes of cities worldwide; they can also help you obtain a big spike in your net cash flow with the proper changes to your structures. Architects play a critical role in real estate development.

Architecture is often looked upon as a subset of real estate development, but the proper and actual relationship of real estate to architecture is not a limiting factor to the services provided. The deeper the understanding the architects have of the real estate development process, the greater value they offer their clients and add to the real estate deal.

An architect designs new structures and modifies and expands existing structures. He or she is legally responsible and has a license issued by the state to ensure that the buildings protect the health and safety of their occupants. Typical questions that an architect can answer authoritatively include:

- How big can I build, and what uses can I put there?
- Can I add any floor area to this existing property, and how would I do it?
- The property is overbuilt, but I have heard about others getting approval to expand. What should I do?
- Can I make vertical additions to overbuilt properties?
- Is it worth it to purchase additional floor area and transfer it to my site?
- The property is in a landmark district. What limitations will I have?
- The property is an IMD building, or the property is an SRO. What are my restrictions?

These are just a few of the important challenges that an architect can help investors to address.

In this chapter, I'll give you five good reasons why architects should play a key role in any New York City multifamily investment strategy. First, you'll learn about zoning analysis, and I'll show you how to effectively "stretch" a building for maximum return. You'll also get the lowdown on how to create new equity by discovering your property's hidden value, followed by a look at the value of "windowless" rooms. Finally, you'll get an insider's view of how to fix a broken deal—something we should all learn more about.

Why Do I Need a Good Zoning Analysis?

With credit tight and the financing of development opportunities being reevaluated with greater scrutiny than ever, a modest investment in an accurate and timely zoning analysis is fundamental to assessing the value, potential, limitation, and risk of any property. The owners, potential buyers, and sellers of properties, as well as brokers, real estate attorneys, and design professionals, can benefit greatly from an illustrated zoning analysis.

Many professionals avoid putting a zoning analysis in writing. However, often the "bulk" cannot be understood clearly without a drawing. Both a written report and drawings are essential. Without them, a proper zoning analysis simply can't be performed and used to the investor's advantage.

A zoning analysis can help answer questions such as: Will a new or future nearby development block a view? Can my property be converted? Can it be enlarged? Can I add a vertical addition? How much floor area is available? What are my density limitations?

In today's market, many buyers are working in the smallest or largest extremes. Numerous developers want to put the largest number of small studio rentals into a property. Some developers, as I have seen increasingly during the past 10 years, want to build family-friendly rental or condominium buildings with larger and larger units, such as three- and sometimes four-bedroom apartments.

People who are buying apartments may see a soft development site next door, in front of them, or two blocks in front of them, and they may want to determine the possibility of how that nearby site could be developed and, if so, what type of building could be put there.

The zoning analysis would study the undeveloped property and inform the buyers or owners who now own or who are considering buying near the development site. For owners or potential purchasers, another consideration is whether a property can be converted from commercial to residential or from manufacturing to commercial. Other queries include whether a property can be enlarged with an addition, up, down, or sideways, and how you can achieve the highest possible market price and/or best potential use of that property.

How to Stretch a Building

Maximizing the value of every square inch of an existing property and adapting to changes in family size and differing lifestyles are trends that are on the rise to keep and attract tenants. To effectively compete for residents, it is desirable for buildings to feature landscaped courtyards, roof terraces, fitness centers, party rooms, and storage facilities. On a regular basis, families are staying put in New York City, not moving out to the suburbs, and combining apartments to gain more space. In order to accommodate these trends, even in "prezoning," overbuilt properties, existing provisions in the building code can be utilized.

Here are three key principles that investors should consider when stretching existing properties:

The "1 Percent Rule"

This rule used to be known as "as of right." It permitted the building department commissioner to increase the floor area of a building by 1 percent of the total beyond what is allowed by zoning. Today, this rule is discretionary. The commissioner evaluates each application case by case. Considerations include the original construction date of the building, the proposed area increase, the proposed use, and consistency with acknowledged socioeconomic trends. A relatively new established trend is the need to enlarge resident managers' apartments to provide for a family. A typical application consists of a letter to the commissioner stating the facts and the request supported by drawings, signed and sealed by a registered architect or engineer. The commissioner can issue a "letter of no objection" and grant the request on behalf of the landlord, board, or tenant. The "1 percent rule" can be used in combination with the opportunities described below.

Provide Access to Inaccessible Areas

Multifamily residential buildings frequently have underused roofs, maid's rooms, subcellars, bulkheads, and tank rooms. Rooftops can be converted to common terraces. The structural roof-loading capacity must be verified because the code requirements for roofs are less than "promenades," the name the code assigns to rooftop occupancies. The certificate of occupancy may also require amending to allow for rooftop use. Raising or lowering the elevator in an elevator building one stop to better reach the roof may sound complicated and expensive. However, when combined with a planned capital expenditure of elevator mechanical upgrades, along with the benefit to the residents of accessing a rooftop that was previously inaccessible, the project may seem less formidable and more desirable.

Handicap access to all building floor levels is increasingly important, whether or not it is required by code. With creativity and careful planning, a building may be able to reuse an existing space in the lower level of a tank room (the water tank is required to be raised 12 feet above the roof level). Former maid's rooms often are underused and can be converted into amenities such as storage, fitness centers, or party rooms. The code does not require natural light and air for these types of ancillary occupancies. Design professionals should be consulted in these projects regarding permits and life safety.

Floor Area Credits for Mechanical Uses

A basic provision in the building code and zoning regulations states that mechanical floor area is not counted toward building floor area. It can be successfully argued and demonstrated by supporting data, calculations, and drawings before a commissioner that successive, incremental air conditioning modifications have used up floor area. Floor-mounted units, duct penetrations, and related equipment, when added together on commercial and residential floors, can be significant. Sometimes, 250 square feet can make a difference and enable a resident manager's apartment to be expanded. Real estate professionals know that buildings are originally constructed for a certain type of user. Over time, the type of user tends to change. It is important to know that owners have options to adapt to these. Learning to stretch an existing building provides flexibility, continued use, and greater value.

"Stretching" in Action
Creating New Equity by Discovering Hidden Value

With the debt market's chokehold on credit, the current prices of real estate are fluctuating greatly, and the sale or financing of new acquisitions is more challenging than ever. Many property owners would welcome the opportunity to increase the value of their holdings. Financiers or potential buyers may want criteria that will help them understand a building's potential future upside when they're determining a property's value.

It is possible to create new equity by researching and discovering the hidden value in existing real estate properties, both commercial and residential, to make them more saleable or more developable and to leverage new opportunities to derive more income from them.

Zoning

Changes in zoning and development regulations can redefine the market potential of any property. Rezonings and up-zonings occur from time to time. A carefully researched update on current zoning information will show what might have changed for that property in that district and determine whether zoning has changed since the time of construction or since the time of the current owner's purchase or what may be forthcoming for consideration for future review by the city's planning department.

For residential properties, architects can establish the available square footage on the lot, the bulk regulation and whether an addition is permissible, the maximum building height and the maximum allowable number of apartment units, or whether "as of right" floor area may be added to an existing building. They can also determine whether New York City's so-called sliver law, which limits towers on lots narrower than 45 feet, applies to the site. The sliver law, which was originally written with Manhattan neighborhoods in mind, applies to high-density residential zones and commercial zones known as C1 or C2.

Development

For a commercial property (hotel, for example), architects can determine setback requirements and possible bonus usage, such as permissible extra floor area for a plaza or a comparable public area. The good news is that development in New York

City is straightforward compared to other cities because most plans can be designed to fall clearly into an "as of right" category.

According to the NYC Department of City Planning (http://www.nyc.gov/html/dcp/html/zone/glossary.shtml), "an 'as of right' development complies with all applicable zoning regulations and does not require any discretionary action by the City Planning Commission or Board of Standards and Appeals," whereas "a discretionary action requires the review and approval of the City Planning Commission or the Board of Standards and Appeals."

Zoning amendments, special permits, authorizations, and variances are "discretionary actions" typically negotiated for you by your architect. Yet, even with discretionary approvals, development can often start with the "as of right" component in place.

The New York City Zoning Resolution, in spite of its complexity, enables "as of right" development in one of the largest cities in the world to be one of the easiest. Here are the basic considerations:

- **The certificate of occupancy (C of O).** Is it out of date? Can it be amended for new use or for the current owner's opportunities? Should it be corrected or updated? The C of O is the key document that certifies the legal use and occupancy of a building and describes how a structure may be occupied. In New York City, according to the Department of Buildings, a C of O is often required when selling or buying a home or refinancing a mortgage. If the planned construction is to create a new building or will result in a change of use, egress, or occupancy to an existing building, then a new or amended C of O is necessary.
- **Open permits and violations.** When someone is planning to purchase a property, he or she might not know whether it's legally encumbered by open permits or "old" violations. Due diligence by the architect for either the buyer or the seller can identify open permits and possible violations that could affect the value or use of the property, its sales potential, or its occupancy. Knowing the negative characteristics of a property can add value so that violations or work that was done in the past improperly or without permits can be corrected now. The result is a more cleanly saleable and, therefore, more valuable property.
- **Landmark buildings and buildings in landmark districts.** There is a distinction between landmark buildings and buildings that are located

in a landmark district. There are also different types of approvals. When approached knowledgeably, the landmark approval process isn't necessarily as difficult as some might think. For work in buildings in landmark districts, the architect must submit relevant drawings of planned changes to the Landmarks Board for review, which can range from staff approval for work that isn't visible from the street to a full public hearing for work that is. Another key service by the architect is to research and present to the Landmarks Board examples of historical precedent for change within the neighborhood.

- **Mechanical deductions.** A mechanical deduction is a way of relocating or moving around floor area in an overbuilt building when it's being converted. The theory is that a new development cannot increase the noncompliance of an existing property. Floor areas currently devoted to air conditioning or ventilation or machine rooms for boilers or water heaters can be measured and added up, and then this total square footage can be presented to the Department of Buildings as "deductible" floor area that isn't being used for actual occupancy. This same amount (not an increase) of floor area can then be relocated, that is, reassigned, to another part of the building for anything from living space to a penthouse or a new elevator. Of course, the relocated floor area must meet the site's bulk requirements.
- **Preconsiderations.** Usually called "precons" in the profession, preconsiderations refer to getting a preapproval before going into the lengthy process of making detailed architectural drawings. Examples of precons are planned changes, replacements, or additions that we want to make sure in advance will be approved. Requested precons are presented to the NYC Department of Buildings for review. If approved, precons can be included with the sale and transferred to the new purchaser of the property.
- **Vertical additions (commercial and residential) and apartment combos.** Even though families or businesses may grow, there is often a wish to "stay put" and remain in the same house or building.

BREAKING

Breaking through and combining two apartments can be accomplished up, down, or sideways, with an architectural design that redefines the total new space rather than just patching units together.

In a residential building where a larger apartment for the building manager or superintendent is desired, a combo breakthrough can result in a much larger apartment by adding adjacent maid's rooms or storage rooms or by using space taken from the cellar or basement. Similarly, the architect can create a caretaker's apartment in a commercial or manufacturing building by creatively carving out and redefining living space.

Wouldn't all property owners be ecstatic if they could discover new, bonus value and hidden equity in their existing properties? The proper architectural analysis can often accomplish exactly that.

A Room with No View

For many apartment dwellers, a home office is an indeterminate breed, a cross between a region of the house and a piece of furniture. Perhaps it begins as a desk with a computer but grows into an unruly beast, covered in papers and power cords, spreading out from a corner of a room used primarily for something else, such as cooking, entertaining, or sleeping.

Apartments with windowless rooms are becoming more common as office buildings are converted to condos. Because each floor of an office building is typically quite large and not designed to have all of its space windowed, there are rooms that simply cannot command a view, no matter how creative the floor plan. The appearance of this new kind of room has also created a new size of apartment, a half-size between one- and two-bedroom apartments. With some priced nearly $500,000 less than similarly sized two-bedrooms in the same building, they come at a half-size price, too.

Still, most home offices are found not in new construction but in conversions of buildings from the turn of the twentieth century.

Everything that is discretionary raises a question, while everything that is "as of right" is straightforward and approvable.

According to the New York City building code, windowless rooms are classified as "occupiable" rooms, such as bathrooms and kitchens, with their own set of rules for ventilation and light, rather than "habitable" rooms, such as living rooms and bedrooms.

The room with no view is a neglected category that many investors could benefit from. With so many people doing at least some of their work from home these days, consider the resale value that comes from being able to put those two little words "home office" on your property listing when it comes time to rent or sell.

Six Ways to Fix a Broken Deal

Whether your project is a "deal" for which construction has already been started and you may need to find out how to make a refi restart, whether you're just now ready to break ground and have experienced chokehold obstacles, or whether you're shopping around, looking over, and evaluating for purchase someone else's existing, faltering deal(s), here are specific remedies for how to fix a broken deal:

1. **Review zoning analysis.** It is important to check how the building was filed. If it was a self-certification that has yet to be audited or if there are still objections, this has to be researched.
2. **Re-review documentation.** It is important to re-review as much documentation as possible, not only filed and approved drawings but also contracts, requisitions for payment, consultant correspondence, and renderings. A fresh review of these documents will reveal the history of the project and may indicate red flags or opportunities passed up for other competing interests that, in a new light, might be valuable.
3. **Compare the design market, then versus now.** Simple. Just this participant design work in today's market or not? You want to monetize your work.
4. **Reevaluate construction cost estimates.** It is both a tricky and a risky task to estimate construction for a building that is not yet finished, especially in a short amount of time, but that is exactly what is required to get some broken deals back on track and going forward again. In addition to looking at the documentation, you have to be able to understand the site logistics of materials handling and where to start over, if necessary, from scratch.
5. **Reevaluate the existing design consultant team.** One must consider carefully the advantages and disadvantages of continuing with the same architecture team. In some cases, the design is so unique to a particular

designer that if the new owner wanted to make fresh modifications, the original designer would possibly be hostile and fight modifications to the design. Sometimes it is better to start fresh and slow down progress with a new team—and no backstory history—in order to see the project from a fresh and more manageable perspective.

6. **Schedule a fresh planning or replanning phase.** Estimating a schedule is as tricky as estimating construction costs. Fight for a robust planning phase. Sometimes an extra month up front will save much more valuable time on the back end. It's important to slow down and untangle the previous knots of decisions regarding design, architecture, engineering, Department of Buildings' expediting and filing strategies, and drawings for steel, concrete, elevators, slab openings, windows, and exterior walls, all of which are important in order to move the project forward efficiently.

With architecture, there is a lot of value out there. While broken deals sometimes look messy and unattractive from a distance, a careful problem-solution approach to the details can often reveal a valuable opportunity in the form of a diamond in the rough.

This chapter includes contributions by Steven Kratchman, president of Steven Kratchman Architect, P.C.

7
Winning the Buying and Selling Game

No real estate is permanently valuable but the grave.

—Mark Twain

To succeed in the New York City real estate market, you have to become the kind of buyer who can identify good properties and act quickly. Unlike other markets, where putting down a deposit and taking the next 60 days to do your due diligence or "homework" (and withdraw the offer and get your money back if the deal isn't satisfactory) is commonplace, New York investors have to educate themselves in advance.

When you sign a contract on a piece of property in New York City, often any earnest money you put down is nonrefundable. Your money goes into risk on day one, even before you officially take ownership of the property. You don't have the luxury of signing on the dotted line and then hoping that all of the gaps get filled in during the due diligence period.

Instead, you'll do the due diligence while you are seeking out lenders, finding partners, and doing whatever else needs to be done to seal the financing. In this chapter, we'll look at how to get everything sorted out before going to contract so you can avoid the problems that come up when you can't clinch the deal. Also you will find tips on the best buying and selling methods and show you how to source a project and close the transaction.

Doing Your Homework

You might pay too much for what looks like a prime property, or maybe you will undersell an apartment building that you've owned for a short time. Avoid both situations at all costs by getting yourself up to speed on the nuances of the transaction before attempting to do business in the city.

Whether you want to be a trader or a long-term owner, you'll face many of the same challenges in the New York City real estate market. Unlike other markets, where apartment buildings vary in age, most of the city's stock was built in the early 1900s. This poses a challenge during the due diligence phase, when boilers, wood-joist structures, and brick facades must be inspected carefully.

In your corner is the fact that when these buildings were constructed, many of them shared the same characteristics. The pipes are all comparable in age, and the electricity was run the same way. You can trace different builders from that time period who built multiple buildings all around the city and see that the buildings are alike, even though they are 10 or 20 blocks apart. From a due diligence standpoint, these similarities speed up the transaction somewhat, although the actual condition of one building may differ greatly from that of the next.

Art and Real Estate

A lot of real estate investors in New York City are art collectors. I've questioned the link between the two on several occasions and learned that art and real estate are similar enterprises. In both cases, you must be able to see value that others cannot. You have to trust your intuition, do your homework, and hang onto your investment until it's the right time to sell.

There are also differences. You can pick up a piece of art and move it to another part of the country or world, but you can't do the same with real estate. Even so, like an art collector, your vision as a real estate investor should be focused on seeing tomorrow's value today using, research, knowledge, intuition and hard work. Every now and then a little luck does not hurt either.

Get to know these buildings from a physical standpoint—during a short 48-hour inspection period—and you'll be well braced to make the right investment decision. There are myriad Web sites at your avail to help you reach this goal. Government agencies and online portals can provide 80 percent of what you'll need. Here are the best sources of information online:

Department of Buildings
(http://www.nyc.gov/html/dob/html/bis/bis.shtml)

BIS is the Buildings Information System, the Department of Buildings' database of licensee information, complaints, Department of Buildings and Environmental Control Board (ECB) violations, boilers, and property profile and construction application information. The database was put into production in 1984 and supports department functions with respect to:

- Property profile information
- Application processing (application submission, review, and certificate of occupancy issuance)
- Accounting
- Inspections (final construction, plumbing, electrical, and elevator)
- Complaint tracking
- Violation tracking
- Periodic safety reports (report submission)
- Equipment tracking (fire safety, elevators, boilers, facade, marquee, and illuminated signs)
- Trade licensing and contractor tracking

The BIS Property Profile Overview is a summary of construction activity, job filings, PRA/ARA (plumbing applications), boilers, violations, and complaints for a particular address. Here are some other due diligence points that you can research on BIS:

- All the alternate addresses for a property are listed, as well as the number of Department of Buildings property records and the Building Identification Number (BIN), a designation assigned by the Department of City Planning.
- The total amount of complaints filed and violations issued can be accessed, with an indication of the number still open.
- The section labeled "Job/Filings" can be accessed, with an indication of the number of construction applications (jobs) and supporting documents (filings) submitted for a property since the department implemented an electronic application filing system in the late 1980s.

- The site also displays information and designations from other agencies, for example, Department of Finance building occupancy codes and block/lot numbers. There is also zip code information to the right of the address.

New York State Division of Housing and Community Renewal (DHCR) (http://www.dhcr.state.ny.us)

The Division of Housing and Community Renewal is responsible for the supervision, maintenance, and development of affordable low- and moderate-income housing in New York State. The DHCR Web site includes information about:

- **Community development:** Administration of housing development and community preservation programs, including state and federal grants and loans to housing developers to partially finance construction or renovation of affordable housing.
- **Housing operations:** Oversight and regulation of the state's public and publicly assisted rental housing.
- **Rent administration:** Administration of the rent regulation process for more than one million rent-regulated apartments in both New York City and those localities in the counties of Albany, Erie, Nassau, Rockland, Schenectady, Rensselaer, and Westchester subject to rent laws.
- **Policy research and development:** Study of the long-term housing needs of the state and development of appropriate policies.

Automated City Register Information System (ACRIS) (http://www.nyc.gov/html/dof/html/jump/acris.shtml

The Department of Finance collects property taxes and other property-related charges, maintains title records and tax maps, conducts lien sales, and collects real property transfer and mortgage-recording taxes. Finance also values all New York City residential and commercial properties and information on condo/co-op comparable rental income. Tax rates are set each year by the city council and applied to property values to determine each owner's annual tax liability.

On the ACRIS site, you can:

- Search property records and view document images for Manhattan, Queens, Bronx, and Brooklyn back to 1966.
- Compute property transfer taxes.
- Create cover pages and tax forms to record documents.
- Find a property borough, block, and lot (BBL) or address.

The ACRIS site also provides the following information:
- **Valuation/assessment** The property tax year begins July 1. Finance releases a tentative assessment of the approximately one million properties in New York City every January. If there are no changes, the final assessment is released in May.
- **Condominium/cooperative comparable rental income** NY state law requires the Department of Finance to value all condominiums or cooperatives as if they were residential rental apartment buildings. DHCR applies income and expense information from similar rental units to value these properties.
- **Rolling sales update** Buyers and sellers can better understand the value of real estate in New York City by using Finance's rolling sales list. Property transaction information is shown for all five boroughs in many categories, such as sales price, neighborhood, building type, and square footage.
- **Tax reduction and rebate programs** Finance offers programs to reduce property taxes and help build new homes and fix up existing ones.
- **Bills and payments** Every three or six months, Finance mails statements of account showing what is owed on each property.
- **Refunds** Owners can use certain credits in their account to pay past or future charges.
- **Rates and other charges** Finance collects charges and fees issued by many other New York City and New York State agencies. DHCR also offers most of the New York City property tax reduction programs.
- **Property information** At Finance, you can find property ownership and transfers by BBL; mortgage records; information about income-producing properties; detailed tax maps; and other data, such as apportionments and mergers.
- **Recording documents** The Office of Land Records keeps the official record of real and personal property transactions (e.g., deeds, mortgages, mortgage satisfactions, and financing statements, etc.).

New York City Rent Guidelines Board (RGB) (http://www.housingnyc.com)

From this site, you can download research reports, view the rent guidelines, send your housing questions to staff by e-mail, view an RGB meeting schedule and organizational chart, or read publications such as the Attorney General's Landlord/Tenant Guide, DHCR's Fact Sheets for Stabilized Housing, or the Housing Maintenance Code.

Of particular value to investors and owners are the RGB's fact sheets, which cover the following topics:

- Air conditioners
- Appealing a rent administrator's order: petition for administrative review (PAR)
- Collectibility of major capital improvement (MCI) and/or owner individual (OI) rent increases where the rent is reduced because of diminution of services
- Collecting overcharges in rent-stabilized apartments in New York City
- Comparative and alternative hardship
- De Minimis conditions in buildingwide or individual apartment areas
- Demolition
- Emergency Tenant Protection Act (ETPA) of 1974 as last amended
- Eviction
- Eviction from an apartment based on owner occupancy
- Expedited processing
- Fair-market rent appeals (FMRAs)
- Fuel cost adjustment
- Fuel cost adjustment: questions and answers for owners
- Guide to rent increases for rent-stabilized apartments in New York City
- Guide to rent increases for rent-stabilized apartments in Nassau, Rockland, and Westchester counties
- Harassment
- Heat and hot water
- High-rent vacancy decontrol and high-rent, high-income decontrol

- Lease renewal in rent-stabilized apartments
- Major capital improvements (MCIs): questions and answers
- Maximum base rent program (MBR): questions and answers for owners
- Painting rent-controlled apartments
- Preferential rents
- Rent increases for new services, new equipment, or improvements to an apartment
- Rent reductions due to decreased services
- Rent stabilization and rent control
- Rent stabilization lease rider
- Required and essential services
- Security deposit
- Small-building-owners' assistance unit
- Special rights of disabled persons
- Special rights of senior citizens
- Sublets, assignments, and illusory tenancies
- Substantial rehabilitation
- Succession rights
- Termination of rent inclusion of electricity and conversion from master metering to individual metering of electricity with direct payment by the tenant
- Useful life schedule for major capital improvements (MCIs)
- Vacancy leases in rent-stabilized apartments
- Window guards

Did You Know?

By law, all rent-stabilized leases contain the same language, and there is a standard rent-stabilized lease that you're required to use with your tenants. The DHCR provides the forms online at http://www.dhcr.state.ny.us/Forms/Rent.

New York State Unified Court System
(http://www.courts.state.ny.us/courts/nyc/civil/index.shtml)

The online database for "housing court" provides information on tenant actions, complaints, and other issues related to specific properties in the city. The court's housing division handles only residential landlord and tenant cases, while commercial landlord and tenant cases and ejectment actions are handled on the civil side.

Each year, more than 300,000 residential cases are filed in the housing part of the civil court, generally referred to as the housing court. Fifty housing judges are appointed to serve in the court. The judges assigned to the housing part and more than 1,000 nonjudicial employees work together to serve the people of New York City.

With all of this information at your fingertips, there's no excuse for coming to the bargaining table without having done your due diligence in advance. I've seen investors do their homework in just 24 hours and have a successful deal in place before the close of business the following day. Add in a seller who keeps decent records on his or her property, and the due diligence period gets even easier.

Buying and Selling Methods

When you buy property in New York, take the time allotted to get to know the building and its nuances before making an offer. When you sell property in the city, you'll use the same care in analyzing your buyer and his or her capabilities and resources. Successful transactions close in the city every day and involve a wide range of investors—from the solo landlord to the institutional investment firm and everything in between.

Take SG2 Properties, for example. When this book went to press, the company was struggling to adapt to changing market conditions, but it had its heyday in the Bronx during the market boom. In total, SG2 purchased about 5,000 units in more than 70 buildings in the Bronx.

How to Act Quickly

Iris Cantor, the major philanthropist and art-collecting widow of Cantor Fitzgerald founder Bernie Cantor, recently closed on a townhouse built in 1910 located at 11 East 74th Street for $18.125 million. Cantor made the offer three days before the townhouse was scheduled to be auctioned off.

The home was last listed at $20.95 million, after being put on the market for $35 million two years earlier and then undergoing numerous price reductions.

That portfolio included a 2007 joint venture between SG2 Properties and BlackRock Realty Advisors. The firms acquired a 51-building multifamily portfolio in the Bronx for $300 million. The portfolio included 4,000 residential units and 80 retail locations, mostly in the areas of the Yankee Stadium, Grand Concourse, Pelham Parkway, Marble Hill, Mount Hope, Wakefield, Kingsbridge, Highbridge, Norwood, and Fordham Bronx neighborhoods. The properties sold for almost eight times the existing rent roll and were slated for upgrades and renovations by their new owners.

In 2009, SG2 was one of several real estate companies that came under fire for putting their properties at risk of default. In many cases, these firms financed their real estate purchases with investments from private equity groups or with mortgages based on future price increases and loose underwriting standards.

These future price increases were based on increasing rents in rent-regulated apartments, like we have discussed in this book, however the assumptions were too aggressive. If you are using leverage, one should study the property's, rents, tenants, turnover rates, and potential carefully before proceeding. Nobody is perfect, and sometimes the projections do not line up with reality.

One of the best buying approaches I use with clients is the "100-10-1" method for purchasing. Here's how the simple three-step process works:

1. You look at 100 properties on paper.
2. You go out and see 10 of them in person.
3. You bid on one and pursue it.

The theory behind becoming a good buyer is to initially go after a big selection of properties and then narrow that pool down to just 10 "maybes." By process of elimination, you'll further whittle those choices down to a single multifamily property whose characteristics and investment potential truly meet your needs. To be an expert investor, you have to know the market. The surefire method is by viewing everything available in the marketplace (100-10-1).

Another approach is through using a good broker who—if trustworthy and acting in your best interest—can save you an incredible amount of time and bring you up to speed in one day. Either way, market knowledge is critical for success.

> ### Wheeling and Dealing
>
> Successful real estate sales play out across the city every day. Former telecom mogul Michael Hirtenstein's $20-million townhouse at 23 Gramercy Park South recently sold. Hirtenstein purchased the house for $14.5 million in February 2007 and put it back on the market in July of that year for $22 million. In September 2008, while Hirtenstein bought and sold real estate elsewhere in the city, including an $11.495-million condominium at the Plaza, the price of the Gramercy Park South townhouse went up to $25 million and was later cut back to $20 million.

As my partner Joe Koicim says: "it is better to knock on more doors." One of our largest clients, who at periods has purchased between 1 and 2 buildings a month, has his "ear to the ground" in a big way I have not seen before. Constantly gathering information from brokers, bankers, superintendants, tenants, attorneys, managers, rental agents, and competing landlords, his market knowledge is hard to beat and that has given him a competitive advantage in his acquisitions. Any successful investor has to always have his ears open and align himself with a team of trusted advisors who provide good information.

You can use a similar strategy when selling. I call this the "30-13-3" method, and it works like this:

1. A great marketing strategy and insight into the most probable buyers for a particular property yields you a list of 30 different potential investors or buying groups.

2. Negotiate and use the process of elimination to get that list down to 13 investors who have the resources to purchase your property but for either price or terms that are not exactly where they need to be.
3. You and your broker enter final negotiations with at least three different parties to sign a hard, noncontingent contract with a single entity.

You only sell once—might as well do it in a way that gives you choices.

> **SELLER BEWARE**
>
> Some may consider it rude to ask about another person's finances, but in the New York City real estate world, it's perfectly acceptable to question a potential buyer's ability to pay. You'll want to know exactly how the buyer is going to finance the purchase. Your top priority should be to find out exactly where every dollar is coming from before you sign that contract.
>
> The fact of the matter is that if those dollars don't show up, you're not going to close the deal. You're well within your rights to be nosy and find out everything you can about financing before putting too much time into negotiating the deal. If the buyer is reluctant to share a bank statement or investment statement with plenty of liquid assets, red flags should be raised.

Use this selling approach and you'll always be in the driver's seat. You'll have plenty of choices and negotiating leverage and will never be left empty-handed by a potential buyer who backs out of the deal at the last minute.

Sourcing Your Project

There are many different resources to tap when sourcing multifamily projects in New York City. There are brokers, owners, newspapers, online portals, attorneys, and many other entities and individuals who can point you in the direction of potential deals. Here are a few good choices:

- **Real estate brokers:** Extremely knowledgeable about the real estate markets where they work, brokers can guide you through the selection, financing, and closing processes. At the start of the relationship, clearly

define the property you desire, how much cash you have for a down payment, who will pay the brokerage commission and how much it will be, and any important contingencies.
- **Attorneys:** Involved in every real estate deal in the city, lawyers know what's going on in the market and can often point you in the direction of available properties.
- **Title and escrow companies:** These folks deal with the real estate industry every day and are often privy to information concerning available properties.
- **Advertising and classified sections:** The Internet may be taking over as an information source, but many sellers still advertise their properties in *The New York Times*.

The NYC Attorney Network

Because they're required when any commercial real estate sales contract is signed, New York attorneys wield significant power in the market. Attorneys are aware of exactly what's going on in the market and are worth tapping for information concerning potential investments. Just remember: you make the business decisions; they should protect you legally.

If you don't know a real estate attorney, ask good brokers, friends, and colleagues for referrals or check out online sources such as the New York City Lawyer Directory (http://nyc.lawinfo.com). However, make sure you get two or three names and interview each. Some are deal makers, others are not, and you need to hire an advisor who has a business style and philosophy that suits you.

- **Trade magazines:** Industrial journals and those dedicated to the real estate industry often have for-sale listings in them. Some of the most notable titles include *Real Estate Weekly, The REAL Deal, Crain's New York,* and *The New York Observer.*
- **Builders and contractors:** These "people on the street" may have properties available or may know of potential investments.

- **Financial institutions:** Insurance companies, banks, and mortgage firms all have an inside track on the real estate market and may know of properties currently for sale or those that will be coming on the market soon.

Any of these sources can help you locate property, and a few of them can even help you take your investment goals from concept to completion.

Analyzing Offers

You own real estate for two reasons: cash flow and/or appreciation. If it is appreciation you are after, often the success of the *entire* investment depends on the sale. That's when you see the value growth that your property has realized over the years, thus making the exit process just as important as the purchase itself.

> ### They Speak Softly, Carry a Big Stick
>
> You'll encounter all types of property owners in the city, but the toughest negotiators in New York are usually small, soft-spoken males from the Old World. They don't look deceptive, but these characters have burned a lot of investors in the city with their wily tactics. Remember that most tactful negotiators and businesspeople *don't* look like they are—and it's done on purpose. I learned this the hard way by one named "Maks." Beware if you run into him and his big, bushy eyebrows. I am still sore from the beating he gave me.

Selling real estate in New York requires the same amount of due diligence that you used when purchasing the property. To find the right buyer, you need to use the right broker, who has the best platform to achieve the highest price and/or best sales terms. I have a long list of qualifications you should require your broker have before hiring him or her. (If you would like a copy of that list send me an email to my contact email at the end of this book with the subject line "Broker Questions" and I will forward it to you.

Once you have selected a buyer, you'll want to look his track record and financial resources; the options, contingencies, and price; the syndication itself (if applicable); and the buyer's liquidity. Here's a breakdown of what you should look for in each of these categories:

- **Track record:** Consider whether there is an established track record for the investor or syndicate. Do they own other properties? What is their reputation? Have they had past failures in the city's real estate market? What due diligence have they performed so far? Do they have hands-on operational experience?
- **Options, contingencies, and price:** What options are included in the contract? What contingencies is the buyer looking to include? How long will these contingencies tie up the property? (Unlike many other markets, where the normal range is 30–120 days, buyers in New York City have much less time to get this aspect of the deal together.) What pricing considerations will offset any prolonged period that the property is off the market?
- **The syndication:** Is the syndication a public or private offering? How focused is it on this particular project? How experienced are the professionals who are involved in this purchase?
- **Liquidity:** Is there an inverse relationship between liquidity and yield? (Investment that's highly liquid should include a lower yield than one with little liquidity.)

Don't forget to utilize one of the few tax breaks that the IRS affords investors: the 1031 exchange. Section 1031 of the Internal Revenue Code states, in effect, that upon the sale of an investment property or real property used in a trade or business, the owner can use the funds from the sold property to purchase a similar, or "like-kind," property and thus not be liable for capital gains taxes on the proceeds from the initial property.

To complete a 1031 exchange, there are some basic rules that must be followed. See chapter 9 in this book for more information about using 1031 exchanges.

The real estate business is all about relationships, effort, and knowledge. If your broker isn't providing these important elements, then it's time to find a new one. Remember that much of your investment comes to fruition when you sell your property, and you have only one chance to get it right. If you have a bad month in apartment rentals, there's always next month. You can't do that when you sell, so work with the best.

8
Property Management

Did you buy a business, or did you buy a job?

—Peter Von Der Ahe

You're reading this book because you are an investor and a businessperson who places a high value on your time. You're capable of doing everything related to running your investment business, but you also realize that part of becoming a successful entrepreneur requires you to use leverage to your advantage.

As Michael Gerber wrote in his book *The E-Myth Revisited* (1995), you want to think about "replacing yourself with a system." You want to go to work *on* your business rather than *in* it. This is done by answering a few questions that Gerber asks in his book:

- How can I get my business to work but without me?
- How can I get my people to work but without my constant interference?
- How can I systematize my business in such a way that it could be replicated 5,000 times so the 5,000th unit would run as smoothly as the first?
- How can I own the business and still be free of it?
- How can I spend my time doing the work I love to do rather than the work I have to do?

If you are fixing toilets all day, then you're not leveraging yourself efficiently. If you're out pounding on tenants' doors to collect rent, then you're also not using leverage to your advantage. If, however, you are researching oil prices and local rental rates, studying how to shield your investment from risk, and capitalizing on other opportunities, then you're focusing on high-value functions while leveraging the rest of the tasks to competent individuals.

> **DID YOU KNOW?**
>
> Leveraging yourself is the key to maximizing your money and profits in any business and is rooted in a simple concept: get the most done by using the least amount of your own effort. Do this the right way and your potential as a real estate investor will be virtually limitless. You'll also be a member of a select group that opts out of the 8-to-5 job, the 40-hour workweek, and limited salary potential and instead takes the entrepreneurial route to success.

If you're new to landlording, you'll want to learn the ropes of property management on your own first, before leveraging yourself. That means getting an inside track on what it takes to operate and maintain a building, manage tenants, and deal with the bureaucracy that oversees the apartment industry in New York City. Once you've educated yourself on these and other key points, you can outsource tasks to individuals who are well suited for the job and who can make informed decisions on your behalf.

Playing to Win

Why is it that some real estate investors succeed while others fail miserably? The answer is straightforward: those who failed did not have the greatest understanding of what it really takes to operate a building profitably. They bought into the "sizzle" and ignored the "steak," only to find out later that they were in over their heads. You can't forget to do the dishes.

In New York City, multifamily real estate is a hands-on industry where you need to be able to cut through all of the fluff and numbers to figure out what it really takes to operate a building. Looking at the investments that have failed or that are in the process of failing will reveal a group of investors who made unrealistic assumptions about the marketplace. Had they taken the time to gain real hands-on management knowledge, they would have realized that the projected numbers would be impossible to hit.

My "Partner" Won't Let Me

Imaginary. Yes, I'm talking about having an imaginary partner: someone you can blame and who can be your scapegoat when you have to make those tough calls. I've seen the strategy used by owners who have to deal with tenants but who don't want to be known as the "bad guy." In fact, this strategy is often used by smaller-property owners who wear multiple hats (owner, investor, super, property manager, etc.).

If you're hiking the rent up to market rates, for example, you don't want to be the one who comes up with the increase and relays it to tenants. Instead, you'll want to defer tenants to a "partner" who makes the financial decisions.

That partner can be your bank. I have seen owners use the bank as a compelling reason to raise rents, when in fact that bank may have said nothing related to the investors' properties or fee structures. This strategy allows you to go in and push through unpopular rental increases while maintaining healthy relations with your tenants.

Even if you're a landlord who manages just one or two buildings on your own, it can still pay to have tenants who associate your "partner"—and not you specifically—with rent hikes and other bad news.

At the end of the day, having a bad guy on your side gets things done quickly and with the least amount of aggravation.

A high degree of government oversight and the prevalence of rent stabilization make the New York real estate industry even more challenging for the investor, who must be able to navigate the obstacles on a daily basis or risk becoming a statistic. The number of city agencies dedicated to rental housing is enough to intimidate even the most seasoned investor.

Here are a few city agencies that you should be prepared to deal with at some point during your tenure as a real estate investor in New York City:

Mayor's Anti-Graffiti Task Force

The Anti-Graffiti Task Force is a coordinated effort to enforce existing local laws, develop new legislative initiatives, and encourage and aid in the cleanup of graffiti.

Department of Buildings

The Department of Buildings (DOB) ensures the safe and lawful use of more than 900,000 buildings and properties by enforcing the building code, zoning resolution, and other applicable laws. Each year, it reviews more than 60,000 construction plans, issues more than 110,000 new and renewed permits, performs more than 300,000 inspections, and issues 12 types of licenses, registrations, and certificates. It facilitates construction by continually streamlining the permit application process and delivers services with integrity and professionalism.

Department of City Planning

The Department of City Planning (DCP) conducts planning and zoning studies to promote strategic development in communities throughout the city. It also supports the City Planning Commission's review each year of approximately 500 land use applications for actions such as zoning changes and disposition of city property. The department assists both government agencies and the public by providing policy analysis and technical assistance relating to housing, transportation, community facilities, demography, and public space.

Design Commission

Established in 1898 as the Art Commission, New York City's design review agency was renamed the Design Commission in July 2008 to better reflect its mission. The Design Commission reviews permanent works of art, architecture, and landscape architecture proposed on or over city-owned property. The commission also acts as caretaker and curator of the city's public art collection and maintains an extensive archive documenting the history of New York City's public works.

Department of Design and Construction

The Department of Design and Construction (DDC) currently manages a design and construction portfolio of more than $4.6 billion of the city's capital construction projects. Projects range from streets, highways, sewers, and water mains to public safety, health and human service facilities, and cultural institutions and libraries. Through a combination of in-house staff and private consultants and contractors, the department delivers quality, cost-effective projects in a safe and efficient manner.

Economic Development Corporation

The New York City Economic Development Corporation (EDC), a nonprofit organization operating under contract with the city of New York, is the city's primary vehicle for economic development services. EDC serves as a catalyst for public and private initiatives that promote the city's long-term vitality. Through affordable financing, tax exemptions, and low-cost energy programs, EDC helps city businesses gain the competitive edge they need to meet their short- and long-term goals.

Department of Environmental Protection

The Department of Environmental Protection (DEP) protects the environmental health, welfare, and natural resources of the city and its residents. The department manages the city's water supply, which provides more than one billion gallons of quality drinking water daily, serving more than half the population of New York State, and manages 14 in-city wastewater treatment plants, as well as nine treatment plants upstate. DEP also carries out the federal Clean Water Act rules and regulations, handles hazardous materials emergencies and toxic site remediation, oversees asbestos monitoring and removal, enforces the city's air and noise codes, bills and collects on almost one million water and sewer accounts, and manages citywide water conservation programs.

Fire Department

The Fire Department (FDNY) responds to fires, public safety and medical emergencies, disasters, and terrorist acts to protect the lives and property of city residents and visitors. The department advances fire safety through its fire prevention, investigation, and education programs, as well as contributes to the city's Homeland Security efforts. The department responds to more than 280,000 fire- and nonfire-related emergencies and more than one million medical emergencies each year and maintains more than 250 firehouses and ambulance stations.

Housing Authority

The New York City Housing Authority (NYCHA) provides affordable housing to nearly 420,000 low- and moderate-income city residents in 345 housing developments with 180,000 apartments in the five boroughs. Through federal rent subsidies

(Section 8 Leased Housing Program), the authority assists more than 87,500 families in locating and renting housing in privately owned buildings. In addition, the authority provides social services for its residents through 112 community centers, 42 senior centers, and a variety of programs.

Department of Housing Preservation and Development

Using a variety of preservation, development, and enforcement strategies, the Department of Housing Preservation and Development (HPD) strives to improve the availability, affordability, and quality of housing in New York City. As the nation's largest municipal housing agency, HPD works with private, public, and community partners to strengthen neighborhoods and enable more New Yorkers to become homeowners or to rent well-maintained, affordable housing.

Landmarks Preservation Commission

The Landmarks Preservation Commission (LPC) designates, regulates, and protects the city's architectural, historic, and cultural resources, which now number 1,128 individual landmarks and more than 22,000 properties in 83 historic districts and 11 extensions to existing historic districts. The agency annually reviews more than 9,000 applications to alter landmark structures. Enforcement staff investigate complaints of illegal work and initiate action to compel compliance with the Landmarks Law.

Loft Board

The New York City Loft Board resolves issues regarding the legalization for residential use of buildings under the board's jurisdiction (known as interim multiple dwellings, or IMDs), adjudicates proceedings resulting from applications filed by IMD owners and tenants, and enforces minimum housing maintenance standards for IMD buildings.

Police Department

The Police Department (NYPD) is committed to providing a safe and secure environment for the public. The personnel assigned to the department's 76 precincts, 12 transit districts, nine Housing Police Service Areas, and other investigative and specialized units protect life and deter crime while responding to emergency calls and impartially enforcing the law.

Procurement Policy Board

The Procurement Policy Board (PPB) is authorized to promulgate rules governing the procurement of goods, services, and construction by the city of New York under Chapter 13 of the Charter of the City of New York.

Rent Guidelines Board

The Rent Guidelines Board provides information on renewal-lease guidelines for rent-stabilized apartments in New York City.

Department of Sanitation

The Department of Sanitation (DSNY) promotes a healthy environment through the efficient management of solid waste and the development of environmentally sound long-range plans for handling refuse. The department operates 59 district garages and manages a fleet of 2,040 rear-loading collection trucks and 450 mechanical brooms. Each day approximately 11,900 tons of household and institutional waste are collected. The department clears litter, snow, and ice from approximately 6,000 city street miles and removes debris from vacant lots as well as abandoned vehicles from city streets.

> **Watch out for the DSNY. I have a client in the Bronx who owns and manages over 200 units. With one particular building, he was receiving sanitation violations on a daily basis. He could not understand why. To discover, he placed a camera on his street and actually caught a sanitation worker writing faulty tickets. With the evidence in hand, he went to court and prevailed. Never let your guard down in New York. Never.

Board of Standards and Appeals

The Board of Standards and Appeals hears and decides appeals from property owners whose various building and renovation applications have been denied as contrary to law by the enforcement agencies.

Water Board

As in many large cities, the entirety of New York's water and sewer infrastructure is funded by revenue it collects through water and sewer rates. The Water Board is responsible for setting these rates and must ensure that it is able to fund the entirety of the water and sewer system's operating and capital needs, enabling the city to provide clean, safe water to New Yorkers for decades to come and to ensure that the health of the city's waterways continues to improve.

Dealing with city agencies is just one of the tasks that you'll have to deal with as a real estate investor. Whether the Anti-Graffiti Task Force sends out a letter about the spray paint marks on the side of your building, the Fire Department questions whether your building is in code, or the Department of Environment Protection receives a complaint about the conditions at one of your properties, you'll need to be prepared to deal with the inquiries efficiently and effectively.

Gimme the 311

Pick up the phone and dial 311 from any borough within New York City and you'll gain access to all of the city's government services and information in one phone call. It's a straight line to a "live" person, who routes the calls to the specific agency that can address the question or complaint.

That means the tenant who sees a mouse in his or her apartment in the Bronx can dial 311 from a cell phone and instantly make a complaint directly to the city. Whereas in the past that call would be placed to the management company handling the building, a tenant's new path of least resistance is a simple three-digit code punched into his or her phone. This simple phone line has changed the property management business in NY forever.

Created by Mayor Michael Bloomberg in 2002, the municipal information system also has its own Twitter and Facebook pages, as well as a Skype account. Residents can get morning 311 alerts as tweets that they would get if they called 311. The system also integrates Google so users can track down the information they're looking for online.

Building owners have become an unintended target of the 311 system, which wasn't created to be a whistle-blowing tool for tenants but has turned into one anyway. Instead of calling their landlords or superintendents when the sink clogs or the roof leaks, residents are calling 311 and filing complaints directly with the city. This can make building management a very expensive and time-consuming process.

Just the Facts

If you think New York City's 311 system is a joke, think again. Here's how it operates:

- The call center is 45,000 square feet.
- The project cost $25 million.
- The 311 center is staffed by 200 operators, who have language translation services available.
- The center handles up to 15,000 calls a day, or 8 million calls a year.
- Its performance goal: answer 80 percent of calls within 5 seconds.
- There are 6,000 items of information stored in an online database for call takers to access.
- The center uses Siebel's software for call center management, Genesys telecommunications software for telephone call handling, Interwoven software for content management, and a Nortel PBX.
- Calls are handled by operators in "tiers": first-level operators handle general questions, and if the caller needs more help, the call is handed off to a specialist operator, who may enter a call for service for a specific agency.
- All calls are tracked and can be analyzed by time of day, agency, and other criteria to help spot trends.
- If a call results in an incident entry, the caller is given a tracking number for the call and is told to call back later for a disposition, which is entered by the handling agency.
- The police department's 122 precincts are linked to the 311 system so they can monitor so-called quality-of-life incidents, which might be handled by another agency but have a criminal connection.

Even the most common situations have turned into debacles because of this direct conduit, which real estate investors must be aware of when managing their properties. The tenant who sees a mouse and calls 311 about it, for example, will prompt a city agency to write a letter to the landlord and send out an inspector to check the property. In the past, the same problem could have been solved by a superintendent and a good mousetrap.

All 311 calls are logged and recorded and used to determine whether a violation has taken place. Landlords can easily come under attack in situations that were otherwise out of their control. Everyone assumes that the complaints are valid, leaving the landlord little recourse when tenants call to complain.

311 Stories

If you're wondering just how tenants in New York utilize the city's 311 system, here are a few real-life examples:

- **Don't Let the Bedbugs Bite** The bedbug epidemic has hit New York City, presenting a seemingly unstoppable scourge that prompted the city council to create a "bedbug advisory board." Complaints to the 311 hotline shot up by 19 percent in 2008, on top of a 33 percent increase the year before, according to the New York City Department of Housing Preservation and Development.
- **Living on a Construction Site** At the back of the red-brick building, part of the Park West Village complex near West 97th Street and Columbus Avenue, crews had been blasting, digging, and working directly outside and underneath the windows of tenants, turning what is now a three-block-long construction zone into the future site of a 30-story tower with retail space and luxury housing. The construction site has been the subject of meetings of Community Board 7 and the Park West Village Tenants Association, and residents have called 311 to make complaints and raised their concerns on community Web sites. Building Department officials issued a stop-work order for all construction operations at the site, excluding the work being done to repair the wall. Devices to detect movement of the apartment building were installed at the request of city officials. The owners and the construction manager, Gotham Construction Company, were issued violations by the Buildings Department for failure to safeguard the public and property.

- **Neighborhood Blight** From a distance, the Chelsea Espresso Bar at the corner of 7th Avenue and 22nd Street looks promising. Move closer, however, and the defunct cafés entrance appears graffiti strewn and covered in contact paper. On the corner of this residential street, the building has become the bane of neighbors' existence. Many of those neighbors have called 311 repeatedly to lodge complaints with the Department of Buildings.
- **Major Equipment Failure** Jacob Neuman was on his way to school in August when he fell 10 stories to his death. The elevator he was in got stuck, and he tried jumping out of the car onto the next floor but didn't make it. A month after he died in the Brooklyn building, the elevator remained in disrepair, with tenants waiting for it, finding nothing but an empty shaft when its doors opened. Calls were made to 311, the Housing Authority, and the NYPD about the elevator.

To deal with this issue, management has to be on the ball and must be ready to quickly diffuse tenant complaints *before* their fingers reach out to dial those three digits. Ten years ago, a call to some inefficient city agents wasn't that big of a deal. Today, a call to 311 can turn into a major headache for the building owner and/or manager.

It's Your Choice

As a real estate investor, you have a few choices when it comes to property management: you can handle it all yourself, you can outsource some of it to capable companies/individuals, or you can offload the majority of the work (in exchange for a fee) to a property management firm. Which route you take is highly personal in nature and depends on how much time you have on your hands and just how good you are with a hammer and a plunger.

One of your biggest jobs is going to be maintaining and repairing your rental units. This means you will put on a tool belt and hit the street on weekends, ready to tackle projects of all sizes at your properties. If you're not going to be physically at the property every day, then you'll want to consider either starting your own property management company to handle these tasks or outsourcing the job to a competent professional for a fee.

> ### "It's Who You Know"
>
> The people you surround yourself with are important not only for the work that they do but also for the people whom they introduce you to.
>
> When building your team, be sure to include an experienced real estate broker who knows the nuances of the New York City real estate market and who has strong connections in the industry.
>
> The difference between a successful referral and an unsuccessful referral could make or break the investment itself. It could also mean that you'll save $100,000 or more during your first year of purchase.
>
> Remember: it's not what you know but whom you know that can elevate you to new heights in the real estate industry.

Alternatively, you can manage the smaller jobs on your own and offload the larger tasks to those professionals. It's your choice, and it depends largely on your level of "handiness," the condition of your properties, your experience at handling such projects, and how much time you have in your schedule to devote to such tasks.

Building Your Team

Successful real estate investing is all about teamwork. At minimum, your property management team should include:

- A property manager
- A superintendent
- A stable group of reliable contractors and service providers that includes:
    - an electrician
    - a pest control professional
    - a locksmith
    - a window replacement/repair contractor

- a plumber
- a carpenter
- an expeditor
- a landlord-tenant attorney

As a team, these entities will be responsible for the basic tasks listed below, plus any other property-specific issues that need to be addressed:

- **Keeping up the property condition:** Getting the best tenants and commanding the highest rent are the primary goals of property management.
- **Tenant applications and screening:** Require all potential tenants to complete an application and then follow up to verify their employment, rental history, and credit and criminal history.
- **Emergency repairs:** Always have reputable maintenance personnel on call to service emergency repairs.
- **Marketing of vacancies:** Get the word out about an upcoming vacancy instantly. Use signage, advertise in the newspaper, post flyers, offer a modest referral fee to existing tenants, or post it on the Web.
- **Move-in/move-out coordination:** Always plan to get a unit "rent ready" within a day or two after it becomes vacated because when you have tenants ready to relocate, they usually want to move in as soon as possible.
- **Keys and locks:** Change the locks each time you have a turnover in tenants.
- **Learn the laws about eviction:** Know what you must do to evict tenants. If you do find yourself in court with your tenant, you need to be prepared.
- **Keep accurate books and records:** Maintaining a good income and expense history is vital to your rental property business.

Did You Know?

Be sure to account for property management services during your property analysis.

On your cash flow analysis, be sure to include 4–6 percent of the gross operating income to cover potential property management fees, even if you plan to self-manage the property.

A good property management firm can alleviate many of the headaches associated with landlording. There are many to choose from in New York City. One Brooklyn property management firm, for example, offers the following services in exchange for a fee:

MAINTENANCE SERVICE
- On-call access to knowledgeable, proactive professionals
- Project management
- Access to a reliable network of professional craftspeople
- Contract supervision
- Periodic maintenance with owner approval
- Management of cost of repairs and projects
- Preventative maintenance and periodic routine inspections
- Routine seasonal maintenance
- Review and evaluation of security
- Assessment of apartments' need for repairs or improvements
- Efficiency testing to identify cost-savings opportunities
- Sanitation

PROPERTY IMAGE
- Moving garbage and recyclables to the curb twice weekly
- Ice and snow removal
- Cleaning of indoor and outdoor areas
- Basic services (e.g., lightbulb replacement, etc.)

FINANCIAL SERVICES
- Collection
- Accounting and bill paying
- Monthly financial reporting
- Budgeting and monitoring
- Tax accountant preparation

OTHER SERVICES
- Violation processing
- Insurance tenant application processing and background checking
- Lease and related document drafting and execution
- Response to governmental documentation requirements

- Tax certiorari (the legal process by which a property owner can challenge the real estate tax assessment on a given property), abatement and assessment, reduction processing
- Evaluation and management of legal matters

There's a lot that goes into running even the smallest apartment building in New York City; aligning yourself with someone who knows the terrain is vital to investment success. To avoid the "hands-on" approach, many investors elect to purchase only buildings above a certain size, or that produce enough cash flow to cover full time professional management. This is to prevent those midnight phone calls on a Sunday from the tenant who needs help changing a lightbulb. Your strategy will be personal as everyone's appetite and capability for the levels of involvement are different.

Just the Facts

New York City law states that any building over 12 units that has an owner who does not reside in the building must have a super on the property 24-7 or a super that lives no more than 200 feet away.

In many New York City apartment buildings, those tenant calls are routed to a superintendent who often serves as the building owner's and manager's best friend. A superintendent may have the responsibility of an entire building crew, including handypersons, porters, a concierge, and other staff. He or she serves at the top of the maintenance operation and reports to the property manager and/or owner, depending on the chain of command.

Get Your Supers up to Speed

Superintendents have many educational opportunities to expand their know-how and enrich their experience, including building maintenance courses and the Superintendent/Resident Manager I and II certification programs offered by SEIU Local 32BJ, the tristate area's building service union.

continues ▶

The union also runs the New York Safe and Secure program, which provides building service employees with four hours of security awareness training to teach employees to be aware of suspicious behavior and packages and what to do in case of a building emergency.

The Department of Housing Preservation and Development (HPD) offer programs such as the Fundamentals of Residential Property Management Series and Intermediate and Advanced Residential Property Management and Maintenance Series. These courses are described as being targeted toward people who are interested in gaining in-depth knowledge about the management and maintenance of multifamily residential properties.

The fundamentals series coursework includes classes such as Introduction to Building Systems and How to Safely Use and Maintain Construction Tools. Intermediate courses include Maintenance of Building Systems/Physical, Building Finance, Working with Tenants, General Construction, Hands-on Electrical Systems, and Hands-on Plumbing Systems.

Upon completion, participants can obtain a Certificate in Advanced Building Management and must complete a specific number of courses/seminars, including Fair Housing, Water and Energy Conservation, and Environmental Health for Owners/Managers.

Many of the prewar brick buildings in New York City come with space dedicated to "super" housing. These apartments usually comprise two- to three-bedroom units built specifically for the super to live in with his or her family. This is where the rubber really meets the road in New York, where the city's old buildings are especially prone to busted pipes and electrical outages. Rather than being indebted to Mrs. Tenant for $85 worth of groceries that went bad in her fridge during the 10-hour power outage, wouldn't you rather have a super in the basement who knows what he or she is doing?

Unless you're the type who can handle such crises on your own, the answer is probably "yes." Ask yourself the same question in regard to the property management responsibilities, which include the hiring, firing, and taking care of the super, the person who can make your building run like clockwork—or not. If your tenants like the super and if they call him or her first before calling 311, then your real estate investment career will run smoothly and more profitably because a good super can save you thousands of dollars a month in repair bills.

"Super" Personalities

Superintendants are an interesting breed, and each of them has his or her own individual personality traits. While in Washington Heights recently, I was working with Rafael, a superintendent for four buildings that I was selling for one of my longtime clients.

We were talking out on the sidewalk, waiting for the investors to show up, when two *boricuas* (Puerto Rican women) strutted by in the 90-plus-degree heat in their black clothing, big earrings, and thick makeup.

They got Rafael's attention. "They are my lobsters!" he shouted, between whistling and howling at the two women. Curious, I asked him what he meant by "lobsters." He smiled, slapped his ass, and said, "I call 'em lobsters because they keep their meat on their tails!"

Landlord-Tenant Relations

By selecting New York City as your investment target, you've chosen one of the most litigious and regulated markets in the country to work in. Great fortunes can be amassed here, but they can also be diminished by a hyperbureaucratic market where rent stabilization, government oversight, and tenants' rights can wreak havoc on real estate portfolios.

The housing court section of the New York City Civil Court was established in 1973 to enforce state and local laws regulating housing maintenance standards in New York City. As such, lawsuits to collect rent, evict people, or enforce state and local laws regarding housing conditions are brought to housing court.

Did You Know?

You can find out everything you want to know about the city's housing court online at: **http://www.courts.state.ny.us/courts/nyc/housing/index.shtml**.

Such Cases Include:

Cases brought by tenants. There are three main types of cases a tenant may bring against landlords:

1. **Illegal eviction proceedings.** The tenant asks the court to order the landlord to let him or her move back into the apartment if he or she was illegally evicted. It is illegal to lock a tenant out of an apartment without bringing a proceeding in housing court. However, there are special exceptions involving orders of protection and squatters/licensees who have not lived in the apartment longer than 30 days and from whom you have not accepted any rent.

> **JUST THE FACTS**
>
> Consult with an attorney before attempting to lock someone out of an apartment. Lock someone out of an apartment that you have accepted as a tenant without coming to housing court and there may be liability for triple the damages the tenant has suffered as a result of the lockout. There may also be liability for damages for wrongfully removing possessions

2. **Housing part ("HP") proceedings.** The tenant asks the court to order the landlord to make repairs in the apartment or building.
3. **7A proceedings.** One-third or more of the tenants in a building with six units or more ask the court to take control of the building away from the landlord and give it to a court-supervised administrator. If the tenants win, an administrator is appointed and collects the rent and makes repairs.

Cases brought by landlords. There are two types of cases a landlord can bring against a tenant:

1. **Nonpayment cases.** The landlord claims the tenant owes rent. The landlord sues to collect the overdue rent and to evict the tenant if the tenant does not or cannot pay the money.
2. **Holdover cases.** The landlord wants the tenant evicted for other reasons besides nonpayment of rent. For example, if the tenant has violated a lease

provision, illegally put others in the apartment, has become a nuisance to other tenants, or is staying after a lease has expired, the landlord may bring a holdover case.

The good news is that dealing with the bureaucracy of housing court generally requires no more than a sixth-grade education. The bad news is that not following the rules will nearly always cost you money, and someone has to do it. A tactical approach tends to work best, and it often pays to put your ego aside and lose a battle in the housing unit yet win the war in court.

Picking Your Battles

If you can run your building by staying out of landlord-tenant court, do it. If you can solve the problem with a small amount of money and none of your valuable time, then go for it. It's usually a better route than going to court and trying to get every penny out of it.

Who your tenants are will determine whether you want to go to court. If you're dealing with high-class luxury tenants, then you'll want to go the distance in court. If your tenants are rent stabilized, then do whatever you can to stay out of court because the rich landlord doesn't win.

Housing court lawyers and judges are notoriously pro-tenant. It's not uncommon to take a tenant to court who hasn't paid rent in six months and have the judge give him or her another three months to pay the balance due. As the clock ticks, it's costing you $1,500 in legal fees for a landlord-tenant attorney, taking up your time, and inflicting emotional stress.

Working with Expeditors

In New York City, expeditors are privately employed individuals who are given the ability to file plans, permits, and paperwork licensees and registered professionals who conduct business with the Department of Building (DOB) on behalf of the expeditor's clients. The real estate industry, including owners, developers, attorneys, architects, interior designers, etc., relies on these individuals for their expertise on codes and DOB procedures to carry a project through to completion.

Did You Know?

The New York Association for Code Consultants (NYACC) is the professional organization that represents expeditors. NYACC also serves as an educational forum to further educate members about the continuously changing requirements, regulations, and procedures of the DOB as well as recent interpretations of zoning and code issues.

Without expeditors, or "code consultants," the time frame would be substantially increased, if the project could be completed at all. Owners and developers who have consulted with architects or engineers about renovation projects, for example, have often found that they needed the assistance and expertise of an expeditor in order to process a project.

Here are the services that expeditors would provide to owners and developers:

- Assist architects and engineers in obtaining approvals for projects at the DOB.
- Obtain all necessary permits.
- Conduct research at the DOB for architects, developers, and owners.
- Provide the zoning analysis for new buildings and additions to existing buildings.
- Cure building violations.
- Obtain certificates of occupancy.
- Obtain place of assembly permit, required for establishments with occupancy in excess of 75 people, such as nightclubs, restaurants, etc.

Expeditor Gone Awry?

Beware of the expeditor who promises too much too quickly. It was announced that the president of an expediting business was recently arrested in New York on charges of faxing a phony document to her client, an architect, to make it appear that the DOB had approved the architect's construction job when it had not.

According to the criminal complaint, in November 2008, a Brooklyn-based architect hired the expeditor's company to accelerate the filing of necessary documents with the DOB.

After receiving repeated complaints from the architect about her company's delay in filing those documents, the expeditor faxed the architect a purported printout of the DOB's Web page and falsely stated that the DOB had approved the architect's submitted application for a residential construction job in Brooklyn.

The architect later received the necessary approval from DOB to renovate the building's interior.

The fact that expeditors are prevalent in the New York City market underscores the fact that real estate is about not only property, financing, lifestyle, and creativity but also relationships, whom you know, and whom you don't know—all of which can either make or cost you money, depending on how you approach the task.

Conclusion

The goal of this book is not only to expose you to the best strategies for New York City real estate investment but also to give you insights into some of the other opportunities in the market. Whether they are upgrading their properties (and in need of an architect), selling their apartment buildings (and in need of financial planning and wealth preservation assistance), or branching out into other areas of the market (and looking for assistance with triple-net leases), the most successful real estate investors collect a vast amount of contacts and information for future use.

It's time to turn your attention to our contributing authors, who can walk you through these and other complex topics. They are all pros who have spent decades working in triple-net leases and estate-planning financial services. Read on for more insights into how you can use their expertise to hone your individual real estate investment strategies.

9
Net-Lease Investments
By Glen Kunofsky
Senior Vice President Investments
Senior Director, National Retail Group

When discussing the net-leased real estate investment in the context of all real estate investment opportunities, it is important to understand where this type of investment lies within the broad spectrum of real estate opportunities. On the active end of the real estate investment spectrum is the owner/manager commercial real estate investment class.

At the other end of the spectrum is the stock acquisition class, the most passive means of real estate investment. This includes investing in the stock in a publicly traded company or a private company that owns real estate, including stocks in real estate investment trusts (REITs). In this type of real estate investment, investors usually earn a fixed quarterly or annual dividend and monitor their investment through quarterly or annual portfolio reports on their holdings.

On the spectrum of the active versus passive real estate investment, the net-leased-investment opportunity lies in between the middle of the spectrum and the stock acquisition class end of the spectrum. There is a popular misconception that because of the nature of the net-leased investment (which we will cover in depth later in the chapter), there is no need to actively manage these assets and no opportunity for gain above and beyond the set annual rent figure. As you will learn throughout this chapter, this is simply not the case.

The Single-Tenant Net-Leased (STNL) Investment from a Money Management Standpoint

It truly surprises me how many money managers fail to acknowledge real estate as a class of assets in the same manner as stocks, bonds, and money market instruments. Way too often I come across clients who have professional investment advisors, money managers, or CPAs who are simply unaware of or don't inquire as to their clients' exposure to different types of real estate holdings. The culture in America is so entrenched in land ownership as a status of "making it" in this country, yet many of the asset managers I meet fail to realize that the majority of most Americans' net worth is tied in some manner to real estate.

For this reason, it is extremely important that you consult accredited investment advisors with proven track records in their field before you enter into a commercial real estate investment of any kind. I usually recommend to my clients creating a "team" when assessing whether to acquire or dispose of any investment real estate.

The team usually consists of a client's real estate advisor/broker, attorney, and CPA. This team approach is no different from the team of professionals that most institutional investment firms employ when making investment decisions. These institutional firms usually have investment committees that make decisions on all major issues affecting the firm's real estate holdings. This team approach allows the private investors to get input and perspective regarding investors' current properties and any potential acquisition properties.

Risks associated with acquisitions vary greatly depending on the investor and the transaction but can often range from market risk, which a broker can best assess, to legal risk, which a client's attorney can best assess, to financial risk, which a client's CPA can best assess. Although this may sound like overkill, it is always better to be safe than sorry. As markets become more and more volatile today, it is extremely important that you have access to the most current real-time market data.

As you will learn later in the chapter, knowing the market in which you invest is key in making the most optimal real estate investment decisions. It is in this capacity that real estate investment advisors can add the most value. Investment advisors are integral in helping you make key decisions in evaluating any real estate decision, whether it be to buy, sell, or refinance. A market assessment of your real estate holdings should be conducted annually not only because of the constantly changing market environment but also because of various "trigger effects." The most common of these trigger effects include loans coming due, unsolicited offers, and the expiration of leases, as well as a change in the owner's investment goals.

> **QUESTIONS TO ASK YOURSELF WHEN EVALUATING YOUR REAL ESTATE PORTFOLIO**
>
> 1. What are my cash flow needs today?
> 2. What are my long-term goals for each asset I own?
> 3. What do I have time to manage?
> 4. Are individual assets likely to appreciate or depreciate?
> 5. How do my investments affect my individual and portfolio income tax, and how does my basis in each property affect estate tax issues?

History Lesson

When you think about it, nearly every war over time has been fought over the same thing: real estate. From a historical context, real estate has been the most important commodity to all prospering countries and is an essential tool for developing countries.

Take New York, for example. The popular legend has it that Peter Minuit purchased the island of Manhattan from the Lenape people in 1626 for $24 worth of glass beads. In fact, Minuit paid 60 guilders, equivalent to approximately $1,000 in 2006 dollars, for the whole island. The lesson to be learned here (besides that you should do your own due diligence and not take all facts as truths) is that real estate historically appreciates over time.

As real estate markets rapidly appreciate, much like the real estate environment of the early 2000s, investors begin to stray from real estate valuation fundamentals and instead begin to chase returns associated with speculative buying. Some investors become averse to investments that seem as simple as a net-leased investment, where the only upside appears to be a set and quantifiable income stream. Instead, they engage in purchases that are tied in no way to inherent real estate metrics and are solely fueled by the potential to sell the property for a significant profit in the short term or even in the long term.

A simplified example of this is the condo boom in the southern Florida market in the early 2000s. For example, an investor would purchase a condo for $500,000 with no regard for what the condo could be rented for and instead expected that the property could be turned around and sold for a 30–40 percent return the following year. This is certainly not the norm.

In a normalized market, prudent investors see that a quality net-leased investment is a prudent and sound strategy. With a net-leased investment, the investment strategy is focused on the present. What is the return on my investment in the current market environment? What potential upside does the market I am investing in provide me in the future? Hopefully, the following chapter gives you an overview of the different types of net-leased properties, as well as a sound understanding for why investing in these properties may complement your portfolio.

Glossary of Net Lease Terms

CAP rate: The ratio between the overall net operating income of the property and its capital cost (essentially the price paid for the asset). For example, a property with a net operating income of $100,000 purchased for $1,000,000 would yield a 10 percent capitalization rate (CAP rate).

Credit tenant: A tenant (e.g., Home Depot, Burger King) whose credit is rated by the major ratings agencies. Properties with a credit tenant generally sell at a premium compared to noncredit tenants (typically franchisees).

Ground lease: A lease in which the landlord owns only the ground on the property and not the building. The tenant then leases the ground from the owner. In this scenario, the landlord is not able to reap depreciation realized on the building. An advantage to the ground lease is that the tenant typically improves the land at his or her own expense. At the end of most leases, the tenant usually but not always leaves the building on the land. Because rent is typically below market, as a result of the tenant just leasing the land, these leases generally trade at a premium.

Leasehold interest: Claim or right to enjoy the exclusive possession and use of an asset or a property for a stated definite period, as created by a written lease. A long-term leasehold interest is a valuable asset in its own right and can be traded or mortgaged as a physical asset.

Single-net lease: Generally, a lease in which the lessee or tenant is responsible for paying property taxes, as well as the rent. The lessor or landlord is typically responsible for any building insurance and expenses incurred for structural repairs and common-area maintenance.

Double-net lease: Generally, a lease in which the lessee or tenant is responsible for paying property taxes and building insurance, as well as the rent, while the lessor or landlord is typically responsible for any expenses incurred for structural repairs and common-area maintenance.

Triple-net lease: Generally, a lease in which the lessee or tenant is responsible for all property taxes, building insurance, and maintenance on the property, in addition to any normal fees that are expected under the agreement (e.g., rent). Frequently used for freestanding buildings.

Cash-on-cash return: The ratio of annual before-tax cash flow to the total amount of cash invested, expressed as a percentage; often used to evaluate the cash flow from income-producing properties.

Net present value: The total present value (PV) of a time series of cash flows; a standard method for using the time value of money to appraise long-term projects; serves as an indicator of how much a particular project or investment adds, in terms of today's dollars.

EBITDA: Earnings before interest, tax, depreciation, and amortization. Essentially, this is a company's cash flow after operating expenses and measures the company's cash flow before noncash charges.

EBITDAR: Earnings before interest, tax, depreciation, amortization, and rent. This is the company's cash flow before noncash charges and rental payments. This ratio is used to calculate coverage ratios (defined below).

Coverage ratio: A ratio used to determine how a company's cash flow compares to its rental obligations; calculated by dividing a store's annual EBITDA by the unit's annual lease expense.

Blended return: The average annual return over the given period of the lease.

What Is a Net Lease?

A net lease is generally defined as a lease in which the lessee (or tenant) agrees to pay some or all expenses normally associated with ownership, such as utilities, repairs, insurance, taxes, and common-area maintenance. A triple-net or absolute-net lease is defined typically as a lease in which the tenant is responsible for all costs and increased costs associated with the operation of the asset, including maintenance costs, taxes, insurance, and structural repairs.

A net lease is thought of in the sense that the rental income is the figure that is net to the landlord after all or some of the expenses are paid associated with the operation of the property. This is in contrast to a gross lease, where the tenant pays a flat figure to the landlord and the landlord then pays all expenses associated with the property. There are many misconceptions about the terminology surrounding net-leased investments.

Way too often investors feel that the nature of a specific lease is derived from whether it can be classified into the single-net, double-net, or triple-net category. In reality, these terms are merely slang terminology created to quickly identify the nature of a specific lease. The true process of creating a lease comes from the product of two parties negotiating a legally binding agreement together. Leases are not as black and white as grouping them into these three categories. As such, I cannot stress enough that any investor must carefully understand the specifics and implications of the terms of the lease prior to investing. Not all net leases are created equally!

How Double-Net Leases Vary from Transaction to Transaction

Many investors believe that in a double-net lease, the landlord is always solely responsible for roof and structural repairs on the property. However, this is not always the case. For example, in most cases, the leases of Dollar General stores are regarded as double-net leases, under which the landlord is responsible for roof and structure. However, in most Dollar General leases, the landlord is also responsible for any piping or HVAC repairs in excess of $500.

Also, something to remember is that each property is different. For example, Dollar General has signed triple-net leases, as opposed to their usual double-net leases, on certain properties where there were limited alternative sites in a certain area and they had to be in a certain geographic proximity for business reasons. Sometimes when the tenant's options are limited, the developer does not have to give in to all of the tenant's terms (i.e., double-net leases vs. triple-net leases).

For example, some tenants refer to a double-net lease as a lease in which the landlord is responsible for roof and structure and the tenant is responsible for all other costs associated with the property. In other cases, tenants refer to a double-net lease as a lease in which the landlord is responsible for roof and structure as well as all plumbing and HVAC repairs that cost more than $500 per occurrence. Although these leases could both be grouped into the double-net category, the natures of these leases have vastly different effects on a landlord's return on investment.

Similar situations arise when addressing real estate tax payment portions of leases. In some cases, the tenant is responsible for all real estate taxes associated with the property, and in other cases, the tenant is responsible for real estate taxes only up to a certain amount of money and the landlord is responsible for the balance and possible future escalations in taxes or assessments. For this reason, it is extremely important to have an attorney, CPA, and broker review any commercial real estate lease before you enter any binding agreement. You may be told the investment is a double-net or triple-net lease, but this may refer to different specifications on a case-by-case basis.

In any market, it is prudent to follow the words of investment guru Warren Buffett, who preaches that investors should always buy what they know. Successful investment in income property is not rooted in fancy models and advanced formulas. The beauty of the net lease is that most investors can easily understand the purpose behind the real estate and can therefore easily see whether the real estate is a good fit for the current tenant. One of the most important aspects of an investor's due diligence is actually going to the site and observing the natural operation of the property. The following examples, although a bit oversimplified, are usually the determining factors in an investor's decision as to whether the property is the right investment:

- **Example A:** An investor visits a Burger King property he has considered purchasing and sits in the parking lot for a few hours during peak and off-peak hours to observe customer traffic flow. The store is packed, and the investor orders a meal for himself and observes that the food is good and the store is well kept. Furthermore, the surrounding area has lots of national retail tenants that drive strong traffic flows through the area. Typically, this is the type of site visit experience in which an investor will ultimately decide to purchase the property if all of the due diligence on the property is satisfactory, including title review, environmental assessments, and review of the tenant financial statements.

- **Example B:** An investor visits a property and observes the location and finds that the site is difficult to access and the store has little traffic. The floor is dirty, the employees are indifferent, and the area surrounding the property has numerous retail vacancies. The investor in this scenario typically decides not to invest in this property even if the other diligence that is done is satisfactory.

The Biggest "No-No" When Investing in Net Leases

The biggest mistake an investor can make is deciding not to visit the site he or she is thinking of purchasing. Just because the site may not require any landlord responsibilities does not mean that it is not important to fully examine what you are purchasing. It would seem that the most logical thing to do when investing hundreds of thousands or perhaps millions of dollars in a property would be to go see it, yet in my experience, many investors don't bother to hop in their car or on a plane and take a look for themselves.

Statements such as "You've seen one Burger King, you've seen them all" or "I am buying the credit of the tenant" are careless and lazy decisions on the part of the investor. Every investor in net-leased property should always assess the investment with the idea in mind that some day he or she may own the property without a tenant in place. Whether this occurs at the end of a 20-year lease or as a result of a tenant default or whether it doesn't happen at all, every investor must be prepared for the worst-case scenario of retenanting the property. For this reason, visiting the property is essential; we all know that the first rule in real estate is "location, location, location."

To succeed, one must not invest in a property for what it could be or what one wants it to be but instead for what it is at the current moment in time. To successfully subscribe to this train of thought in the commercial real estate space, one must always take into account the following five points when underwriting any real estate investment property:

1. **Current cash flow and expenses:** What is my bottom line on this investment?
2. **Market rents:** Is what my tenant is paying the going rate? If something happened to the tenant, could I easily replace this rental income?
3. **Vacancy rates:** Is there an abundance of space to be had in the area? What is the trend? Is demand shifting toward or away from this area?
4. **Debt services coverages:** Worst-case scenario if my rental income takes a hit, what is my ability to pay my debt service?
5. **Demographics:** What are the demographics of the area? Is this the type of area in which the subject property would thrive from a business operations standpoint? Is this a high-end market, where a luxury retailer would thrive, or is this a low-end market, where I should be purchasing a discount retailer?

SIMPLIFIED NET LEASE UNDERWRITING CRITERIA

I. Real estate assessment
   A. Site inspections
   B. Macro and micro demographic analysis
   C. Traffic counts and patterns
   D. Vacancy and alternative use of property

II. Credit analysis
   A. Review of tenant financial statements (balance sheet and income statement)
   B. Credit rating
   C. Years in business of tenant
   D. Principals of tenant (how many years of experience within the company)

III. Unit-level analysis
   A. Review of unit-level profit and loss statements for the unit you are purchasing (three years of historical info if available)
   B. Rent coverage analysis
   C. Review of on-site management (how long management has been at this location)

continues ▶

> IV. Legal and transactional document review
>   A. Title and survey review
>   B. Environmental report and property condition report
>   C. Contract and lease review

Types of Net Lease Properties

Most of this book is dedicated to multifamily real estate in New York City. While this is a topic that deserves a book all to itself, the reality is that most real estate investors branch out into other commercial real estate opportunities as well. The most common net-leased assets fall into the following categories:

Retail

- Financial (bank branches, credit unions, etc.)

Example:
People's Bank, Overland Park, KS
Sold: 6.76% CAP ($5,405,000)

Big-Box Retail

Example:
Home Depot, Bridgewater, MA
Sold: 7.15% CAP ($11,550,000)

Restaurant (fast-food, fast-casual, high-end luxury)

Examples:
Ruth's Chris Steakhouse, Palm Desert, CA
Sold: 6.25% CAP ($5,703,000)

Smokey Bones, Lithonia, GA
Sold: 13.25% CAP ($1,179,547)

Convenience Store (gas station optional)

Example:
Circle K, Raleigh, NC
Sold: 7.05% CAP ($1,470,280)

Grocery (Kroger, Food Lion, Stop 'n' Shop)

Example:
Cub Foods, St. Paul, MN
Sold: 7.5% CAP ($14,000,000)

Office

- Company headquarters (financial services, retail HQ, medical HQ)

Example:
Hartford Insurance Corporate Plaza, New Hartford, NY
Sold: 9% CAP ($17,400,000)

Industrial and Manufacturing

- Textile facilities
- Industrial warehouses and factories
- Production plants

Example:
Hughes Supply Center, Tupelo, MS
Sold: 7.85% CAP ($549,561)

Hotel

- Primarily name-brand operations

Example:
Hampton Inn ground lease, Ormond Beach, FL
Sold: 6.75% CAP ($4,750,000)

Did You Know?

Net-leased rental rates for commercial investment properties are sometimes determined on an EBITDAR/rent coverage ratio. In layperson's terms, this means that the rent for these net-leased assets is set according to a percentage of the unit's annual cash flow before interest, tax, depreciation, amortization, and rent—effectively, its cash flow before noncash charges. Typically, rents are set at an EBITDAR/rent ratio of 1.5 to 2.5 times EBITDAR.

It is necessary to take stock in this ratio for two reasons: first, the credit of the tenant can fluctuate on a quarterly basis and, second, this ratio measures the store's ability to pay rent. Much like banks use debt-coverage ratios, this metric is an effective way to determine your investment's financial viability. Oftentimes, novice investors look at what the unit's rent-to-sales ratio is at a given location when, in fact, this is often not helpful. A property can have an extremely low rent-to-sales ratio and the store can still be losing tons of money at that location.

For the most part, net-leased properties are usually single-tenant commercial, industrial, or office properties with long-term leases backed by a corporate or personal guarantee. These leases usually obligate the tenant to pay the landlord a certain rent, as well as directly pay for real estate taxes, insurance, and building maintenance and upkeep. This is why assessing the strength of the guarantor is an essential element in assessing risk in a net-leased investment. It doesn't matter what the lease says if the tenant can't or won't pay the rent and additional expenses associated with the lease.

Examples of the types of tenants one could expect in each asset class are listed above. The most common types of net leases that are seen in the marketplace are double-net and triple-net leases. What makes one type of property a double-net lease and another a triple-net lease? As described earlier, traditionally, in a double-net lease, the landlord remains responsible for any structural or roof-related repairs that are associated with the property. In these cases, it is important to underwrite a capital expenditure reserve as a landlord expense. Traditionally, on double-net-leased assets, this reserve set aside for CapEx (capital expenditures) is between 10 and 25 cents per square foot, depending on the size of the property and the age of the building.

How Net Leases Originate

Many investors have a perception that net lease properties are designed for investors who want to take advantage of 1031 exchanges, but that assumption is false. There are three different ways that net lease properties end up in the marketplace, where private or institutional investors can buy them. Here is how it works:

Developers

Developers build properties for a living. A developer in a particular market owns land and wants to produce income from that land or generate fees for entitling, zoning, and, eventually, building that property. The developer approaches a tenant (or vice versa), such as Burger King or Walgreen's, and offers to build the location for a certain rate of return. The developer and the tenant then negotiate terms, including pricing, initial rental rate, lease term, escalations, and tenant improvements, as well as various other business points. The tenant signs the lease, and the developer now has an income-producing property. However, most developers rarely hold these properties long term and instead sell them in order to monetize their investment so that they can undertake more projects and continue to roll their money. Developers employ different strategies when using this approach, with most of the properties historically being sold to institutional landlords such as real estate investment trusts (REITs) that had a lot of cash and were in need of future cash flow. They'd buy the property and put it into a large public or private fund. Alternatively, the developer would refinance the property after the lease was in place for all or most of the investment back.

During the past 10–15 years, those opportunities have become more open to private investors.

Sale-Leaseback

In this scenario, tenants seek out locations on which to build their own stores. They purchase the land and develop the property themselves. Rather than keeping that real estate on their balance sheets when their primary business model isn't focused on real estate, they complete a sale-leaseback. In doing so, the owner of a property (the tenant/user) sells that property and then leases it back from the buyer (landlord). The purpose of the sale-leaseback is to free up the original owner's (tenant/user's) capital while allowing retention of possession and use of the property under the terms of the lease.

> ### Why Sale-Leaseback Transactions Make Sense
>
> 1. **They improve the balance sheet.** Operators can free up the capital locked in their real estate and improve their balance sheet at the same time. By selling the real estate, operators can have more cash on their balance sheet while taking a noncore asset such as real estate (and any related debt) off of it. Additionally, lease payments are often considered an operating expense versus a liability and are therefore an off-balance-sheet item.
> 2. **They free up cash.** Executing sale-leaseback transactions can be a less expensive way of obtaining financing for expansion than traditional forms of financing. Often, operators will execute these transactions in order to expand their current operations.
> 3. **They pay down debt.** Oftentimes, sale-leaseback capital is cheaper than equity capital and therefore makes more sense than raising equity and giving up some control of the ongoing business. Typically, a tenant is going to realize a better return on these operations than any appreciation on real estate.

Secondary Markets

The final way in which net lease properties come to market is through the secondary market. These are the transactions where there are an existing property and lease in effect and an owner who is ready to sell. Another investor expresses interest in acquiring the asset from the existing owner. In this instance, the lease is already signed and in place, and a simple assignment of the current lease occurs, along with the ownership of the land changing hands.

The Rationale

One reason people choose to invest in net lease properties is diversification. Net-leased investments allow investors to reach out of their immediate geographic area and put money into properties they wouldn't necessarily, if the property required a more management-intensive strategy.

Such diversification is particularly apparent when property values in specific markets are in decline. If all of an investor's real estate holdings are in one concentrated area, the investor is completely exposed to the fluctuations of that specific market. Through a strategy that employs geographic diversification, the investor has the ability to now spread risk throughout a wide variety of markets. It is in this sense that the net-leased investment is very useful. It allows investors to reach out of their immediate geographic location and diversify their risk across various markets as well as property types.

Net leases are very basic in nature. Return on investment is easy to predict and is based on current cash flow and credit. Net lease returns are largely rooted in the present returns, not in speculative returns that may or may not be realized. It is in this sense that net leases are valuable tools. Investors essentially trade some of their upside for a quantifiable and predictable future return. Net leases lay out exactly what one is investing in, what the rents are going to be on an annual basis, and what those increases are going to be over the entire lease period. If investors do their diligence on these investments and understand the risks associated with each property, they can achieve predictable long-term cash flow. People invest in them primarily for cash flows and less for appreciation.

Owners of quality net lease properties don't have the same responsibilities on a daily or monthly basis as hands-on managers do, nor do they have to directly stress over skyrocketing expenses. In New York City, for example, expenses such as real estate taxes, oil, and utilities are constantly on the rise. Combine these rising costs with governmental regulation and rent stabilization and the ordinary investor finds that his or her investment is not exactly subject to a "free-market" system, as in other markets. In a net lease scenario, however, the tenant is generally responsible for any increases, including those associated with property taxes and capital improvements. In the industry, we call this a "100 percent pass-through" to the tenants.

1031 Exchange

The following information is solely the author's take and interpretation of 1031 tax code and in no way should be taken as absolute truth. The author is not a CPA and does not claim to be one, so it is imperative that you consult your CPA and/or attorney to make sure you are in compliance with current tax code before engaging in or initiating a 1031 exchange.

The 1031 tax-deferred exchange is a powerful tool within U.S. tax code that real estate investors can use to grow their income and diversify their portfolios. In a typical sales transaction, the property owner is taxed on any gain realized from a sale. However, through a Section 1031 Exchange, the tax on the gain is deferred until some future date. A 1031 deferred exchange is a section in the tax code by which a property owner trades one or more relinquished properties (down-leg) for one or more replacement properties (up-leg) of "like kind" while deferring the payment of federal income taxes and in most states the state capital gains tax as well as depreciation recapture.

Tax-deferred exchanges have been a part of the tax code since 1921 and are one of the last significant tax advantages remaining for real estate investors. One of the key advantages of a §1031 exchange is the ability to dispose of a property without incurring a capital gain tax liability, thereby allowing the earning power of the deferred taxes to work for the benefit of the investor (exchanger) instead of the government. In essence, it can be considered an interest-free loan from the IRS.

IRC §1031 (A)(1) states:

"No gain or loss shall be recognized on the exchange of property held for productive use in a trade or business or for investment, if such property is exchanged solely for property of like-kind which is to be held either for productive use in a trade or for investment."

PRACTICAL USES OF THE 1031 EXCHANGE

- **Example 1: Deferring a Capital Gain to the Next Tax Year** If the sale of a property occurs within the last 180 days of a given year, an investor can put his or her money into a 1031 exchange account with an accommodator. Even if the 1031 exchange is not successfully

- completed, the capital gain will be deferred to the next tax year, when the investor receives funds from the "blown" exchange. Investors have used this strategy when they know about losses they may have in the next tax year. In this case, investors then use that anticipated loss to help offset the capital gain they recognized in their first transaction.
- **Example 2: The 1031 and Tax-Friendly States** Some investors have used 1031 exchanges to ultimately defer their capital gain when they anticipate relocation to a state that has a lower tax rate than the state they currently reside in. As this relates to New York investors, many New Yorkers have planned to retire in Florida, where there is no state income tax. By deferring the gain until the investor becomes a permanent resident of Florida or a similar state, this would effectively eliminate the state portion of his or her capital gains by deferring the gain until he or she has established permanent residency.

Section 1031 tax-deferred exchanges continue to increase in popularity as more investors nationwide discover the wide range of investment objectives that can easily be met through exchanging, including:

Preservation of Equity

A properly structured exchange provides real estate investors with the opportunity to defer 100 percent of both federal and state capital gain taxes in states that fully recognize the federal code. This essentially equals an interest-free, no-term loan on taxes due until the property is sold for cash. Most often, the capital gain taxes are deferred indefinitely because many investors continue to exchange from one property to the next, dramatically increasing the value of their real estate investments with each exchange.

Leverage

Many investors exchange from a property where they have a high equity position or one that is "free and clear" into a higher-priced property. Sometimes, a higher-priced property raises the investors' tax basis on the new asset they have acquired but also can produce greater cash flow and therefore provide greater depreciation benefits, which therefore can increase investors' after-tax return on their investment.

Diversification

Investors have a number of opportunities for diversification through exchanges. One option is to diversify into another geographic region. For example, an investor may exchange out of one large big-box retail space in Denver for two smaller retail properties, one convenience store in Los Angeles and one quick-service restaurant in Dallas. Another diversification alternative is acquiring a different property type, such as exchanging several residential units for a small retail strip mall.

Management Relief

Many investors accumulate several single-family rentals over the years. Exchanging these properties for one property better suited to on-site maintenance and management can lessen the ongoing maintenance and management of what can be a far-reaching group of properties. Exchanging into a net-leased property or even a single apartment complex with a resident manager is a good example of this strategy.

Estate Planning

Often, a number of family members inherit one large property and disagree about what they want to do with it. Some want to continue holding the investment, and some desire to sell it immediately for cash. By exchanging from one large property into several smaller properties, an investor can designate that, after his or her death, each heir will receive a different property that can be held or sold.

The IRS allows up to a maximum of 180 days between the sale of the relinquished property and the purchase of the replacement property. During this 180-day "exchange period," the investor must also properly identify suitable replacement properties within 45 days of closing on the sale of the relinquished property. Here are the basic requirements that must be met in order to qualify for a tax deferral under the tax code:

1. Both the "relinquished/down-leg" and "replacement/up-leg" properties must be held for investment or used in business. The IRS uses the term "like kind" to describe the type of properties that qualify. Any property held for investment can be exchanged for any other "like-kind" property held for investment. This definition covers a vast variety of developed and undeveloped real estate. Properties that are clearly not like kind are an investor's primary residence or property "held for sale." The relinquished and replacement properties need not have identical functions (i.e., both be residential rentals or commercial strip centers). The key issue is that the exchanger can substantiate that both the relinquished property and the replacement property were "held for investment" or "used for business."
2. The IRS requires an investor to identify the replacement property (or properties) within 45 days from closing on the sale of a relinquished property. The 45-day identification period begins on the closing date, and the replacement property (or properties) must be properly identified in a letter signed by the exchanger (the seller) and received by the qualified intermediary (see requirement 4 for explanation). Although the exchanger can identify more than one replacement property, the maximum number of properties that can be identified is limited to using one of the three rules below in order to identify potential exchange opportunities:

    - **Three-property rule:** Investor may identify up to three target properties without regard to their fair-market value.
    - **200 percent rule:** Investor can identify an unlimited number of replacement properties if the total fair-market value of all the properties is not more than twice the value of the property sold.
    - **95 percent exception:** Investor can identify any number of properties without regard to the combined fair-market value, as long as the properties acquired amount to at least 95 percent of the fair-market value of all identified properties.

3. Close on the replacement property by the earliest of either 180 calendar days after closing on the sale of the relinquished property or the due date for filing the tax return for the year in which the relinquished property was sold (unless a filing extension has been obtained).
4. The most common exchange format, the delayed exchange, requires investors to work with a qualified intermediary, who actually documents

the exchange by preparing the necessary paperwork (exchange agreements), holding proceeds on behalf of the exchanger, and structuring the sale of the relinquished property and purchase of the replacement property.

Before investing in income-producing commercial property or engaging in a 1031 exchange, investors should consult with their financial advisors and real estate professionals to make sure that they are making the soundest investment decisions given their individual situations. Deal with professionals who have devoted their professional careers to the industry, and align yourself with investment advisors who understand the value of real estate as an investment class and how it relates to the overall performance of your investment portfolio.

Most important, seek out professionals who know the national net-leased marketplace. You are ultimately investing in your future financial security and do not want your local broker acting on your behalf on a transaction in Tennessee simply because you have a standing relationship with him or her or because he or she is a family friend. Your future financial security is too important. Consult the professionals who are transacting in these markets daily, and in the end, remember that you are not just buying some credit lease on paper—you are buying bricks and dirt.

10

Trusts and Estates
By Mark W. McGorry,
Managing Director, Wealth Partners LLC

As we work our way through the planning opportunities associated with NYC investment real estate, I would like you to keep in mind one of our long-term clients. He is a business owner whose wealth has been developed from the income from that business, his personal investments in financial assets (primarily through tax-qualified retirement plans), and his investments in NYC income-producing real estate.

The business provided a very good lifestyle for him and his family over the years and also served as an engine to generate personal savings. However, ultimately, a very large portion of his nonbusiness wealth came about through the income and capital appreciation from his investments in NYC real property. Some of this property is related to use by his operating business, but most of it came from personal investments, in conjunction with reasonable use of leverage when acquiring and also when refinancing these investment properties.

Our client is one of those people who would never have thought he would be interested in retiring or even slowing down. But at age 65, he is beginning to realize that he might want to change course as he gets older and consider spending at least some of his time in other ways. With this in mind, he has worked with us, conjointly with his other advisors, in developing a comprehensive plan that takes into account personal, financial, business, and estate objectives. Below, you will see how his NYC real estate investments fit into this planning and the opportunities available him with them to meet his objectives.

Historically, real estate has been one of the most common tools for creating personal wealth. There is no reason to believe that this will change in any fundamental way. As the well-worn cliché states, "Real estate: they aren't making any more of it." Where there is a limited amount of a commodity or resource, there is a long-term increase in the value of that item. Plus, unlike many commodities, such as precious metals, real estate possesses unique qualities that provide special financial and tax opportunities for the investor.

An investment in New York real estate is also an asset that is provided some significant tax advantages in the area of income taxes as well as gift and estate taxes. Tax-savings opportunities exist whether you are buying, selling, or holding real estate. In this chapter, we'll review these tax-savings opportunities. As we go through the advantages, you'll need to have a clear view of your own financial situation and a definition of your personal goals.

Typically, a real estate investor has one or more goals in mind in regard to tax planning and real estate. They fall into these categories:

- You want to make changes that can provide greater cash flow.
- You're looking for greater liquidity.
- You're interested in transferring wealth to members of a younger generation.
- You want to minimize income or capital gain taxes.

Using the strategies in this chapter, you'll be able to reduce current and future income and capital gain taxes as well as gift and estate taxes. These tools will prove useful when you are acquiring new property, selling property you've been holding in your portfolio, or planning for the property you will hold for a long time or even for life. The strategies include the use of charitable split-interest transfers, which allow you to benefit from your property while reducing taxes on the sale of the property and minimizing transfer taxes on the same economic benefits you wish to pass to your children.

I'll also show you how to use various types of trusts that are also treated as "grantor trusts" for income tax purposes but not for estate tax purposes. These income tax–defective grantor trusts can be structured to minimize the value of a transfer of the property for gift taxes purposes and even allow you to pay the income taxes associated with the transferred interest without additional gift taxes. The result is an additional increase in value to the beneficiaries and an equal decrease in your taxable estate, without any additional gift tax.

Income Tax Attributes

Real estate investments can offer shelter from income taxes typically in the form of tax deferral. Typically, depreciation and other noncash deductions, in addition to deductible cash expenses, can result in free cash flow that is greater than taxable income. Direct deductions from both cash flow and taxable income include payments for mortgage interest, taxes, and operating expenses.

While payments for mortgage principal reduction are not a deductible item, the noncash deduction from depreciation will often shelter those payments and some or all of the remaining free cash flow from current taxation. At times, these tax losses can even be large enough to shelter other unrelated unearned income or wages from taxation, generally subject to a maximum of $25,000 in a single year, with a carryover to future years or amounts in excess.

In addition, as a property appreciates over time, that growth in value is not currently taxable until the property is disposed of in a sale. It is not uncommon for property owners to remortgage their properties over time in order to avail themselves of cash on a tax-deferred basis. Ultimately, it is possible when disposing of property to further defer tax recognition through techniques such as "like-kind" exchanges (discussed elsewhere in this book), installment sales, or charitable planning techniques.

It's an old joke among tax practitioners that the ultimate permanent income and capital gains tax avoidance plan is death. This is because at the time of death, the capital assets included in the decedent's estate, including real property investments, are "stepped up" in value to the value at death for purposes of calculating capital gain in a subsequent sale by the estate or the heirs. As a result, the investor got all the benefits of tax-free recapture of the investment during life, and the heirs in effect get the same tax benefit again, plus forgiveness of income taxation on all of the lifetime appreciation. All they pay are taxes on post-death appreciation when they sell.

The trade-off to this once-in-a-lifetime income and capital gain tax exclusion benefit is that it applies only to capital assets that are includible in the decedent property owner's taxable estate. At the time of this writing, the amount of estate assets exempt from federal estate tax is $3,500,000, reduced by taxable gifts made during a lifetime.

As a result, it is possible to have assets that are includible in the taxable estate that qualify for both income and capital gains tax elimination benefits associated with step-up in basis and that also escape federal estate tax, if the total taxable estate plus lifetime taxable gifts do not exceed $3.5 million. There are also estate taxes due to New York State. The tax rate starts at about 4 percent after a $1,000,000 exemption and graduates up to a rate of about 16 percent on amounts in excess of $10 million. The result is a partial trade-off between the planning benefits offered by planning for the income tax benefits of step-up in tax basis as opposed to techniques to minimize the bite of estate taxes.

Either way, New York City real estate investing offers some distinct planning opportunities.

Let's assume that the combination of federal, NYS, and NYC capital gain tax rates is 25 percent, depending on whether the taxpayer is in AMT and able to avail himself or herself of the tax benefits of deducting the city and state taxes on his or her federal return. We'll also assume that the marginal federal and New York estate tax rate nets out to 50 percent (it might be several points higher or lower in actuality for a given taxpayer).

We will refer to family members of the oldest generation as G1, their children as G2, and G1's grandchildren as G3.

Let's now take an inventory of many of the planning concepts that relate to tax savings to consider, whether you are buying, selling, or holding real estate.

Family Limited Partnership

Family limited partnership (FLP) can be used for long-range estate planning with investment real estate. The FLP can be a valuable estate-planning tool to reduce the burden of estate- and generation-skipping transfer taxes. It is also a means of protecting assets from creditors.

Typically, G1 will create a partnership and transfer capital assets, such as investment real estate, into the partnership. Within the partnership structure, G1 is the general partner, and G2 and/or G3 are the limited partners.

G1 as general partners often own only a small proportion of the partnership, while the limited partners, composed of G2 and perhaps G3, own the majority interest. The general partners have complete control of partnership activities. The limited partners have no control or management rights.

Some estate-planning strategies must be irrevocable in order to be effective. These irrevocable tools cannot easily be changed or undone. However, the FLP operating document can be modified to respond to changes in the family or business structure.

G1 can contribute assets to the partnership as an estate-planning tool; they are transferring asset value and shifting asset growth from themselves to a younger generation. The partnership can benefit from their experience, knowledge, and contacts in the real estate field to help grow the value for G2 and G3.

The income tax rules governing partnerships are quite flexible and can allow for allocation of income to different partnership ownership interests that do not always have to be in direct proportion to activity level by the partners.

There can also be a creditor protection aspect to partnerships because most state limited-partnership statutes prevent the creditor of a limited partner from attaching partnership assets. While the creditors may get a charging order against the debtor's partnership interest, as a practical matter it is very difficult to collect debt.

Grantor-Retained Interest Trust (GRIT)

These trusts are creatures of statute and to qualify as an effective estate-planning tool must either pay the grantor a fixed payment at least annually (an annuity) or pay a fixed percentage of the trust assets as computed annually (a unitrust). If rights to the income are retained, the value of the remaining interest is reduced, along with the potential gift tax. If the grantor lives beyond the term of years selected to receive the income, the asset will be totally removed from his or her taxable estate.

The **GRAT** is a "grantor-retained annuity trust." By following the rules laid out in IRS regulations, it may allow G1 to transfer assets with growth potential to G2 and G3 with minimal payment of gift taxes.

Here is how it works: grantor (G1) transfers a remainder interest in an asset to a GRAT (irrevocable trust) for a fixed period of years. G1 retains the right to receive a fixed payment (at least annually) for that fixed period of years.

At the end of the designated time period, the remainder passes to G2 or G3 or a trust for their benefit.

The value of the transferred asset minus the value of the retained annuity interest will equal the value of the remainder interest that is subject to gift taxation.

For example:

>Value of asset placed in GRAT: $1,000,000
>Current annual income: 5 percent
>Growth: 3 percent
>Age of grantor G1: 65
>Term of GRAT and annual payment back to G1: $50,000 per year for 10 years
>Federal discount rate (a rate set by the formula by the IRS monthly): 3.4 percent (July 2009)
>Present value of the remainder interest calculated under the regulations: $582,065
>Value of the taxable gift: $582,065
>Illustrated value in 10 years, passing to G2 or G3: $1,447,050
>***Future value removed from estate in 10 years: $868,985***
>***Potential gift and estate tax savings: $434,492***

The cost of the transfer would be the gift tax on the value of the remainder interest of $291,032.

Because this is a gift of future interest, it does not qualify for the annual gift tax exclusion. However, the gift tax on assets up to $1,000,000 is first offset by an individual's applicable credit amount for federal tax purposes, and in New York, there is currently no gift tax. The federal tax on gifts that exceed $1,000,000 must be paid in cash in the year the gift is made and will also be a credit toward the estate tax at the time of death.

When interest rates are low is the best time to take advantage of the transfer tax opportunity offered by GRATs.

The opportunity and benefit are further compounded in times of temporarily reduced property valuations.

Valuation Discounts

In gift and estate planning, as well as real-world transactions, the valuation of an interest in a closely owned business entity, such as a real estate investment partnership or LLC, must recognize valuation discounts for lack of both "minority interest ownership" and "marketability." It is an accepted fact in valuations that a buyer of a minority interest will negotiate a discount because he or she will not have control over the operation of the business. Likewise, an additional discount will be negotiated for the lack of marketability that generally exists for an interest in a closely held business for which there is not a regular marketplace to sell that interest.

The combined level of these discounts for a minority interest in a real estate investment business can easily be from 20 to 35 percent, or even up to 40 percent.

For this example, we will use the fairly conservative 20 percent discount:

> Value of asset placed in GRAT: $1,000,000
> Current annual income: 5 percent
> Growth: 3 percent
> Transfer tax value after 20 percent discount for minority and lack of marketability: $800,000
> Age of grantor G1: 65
> Term of GRAT and the annual payment back to G1: $40,000 per year for 10 years
> Federal discount rate: 3.4 percent (July 2009)
> Present value of the remainder interest calculated under the regulations: $465,650
> Value of the taxable gift: $465,650
> Illustrated value in 10 years, passing to G2 or G3: $1,447,050
> ***Future value removed from estate in 10 years: $981,400***
> ***Potential gift and estate tax savings: $490,700***

Client Update

Some years ago, our client, now 65, began to move his NYC investment properties into a limited-liability company (LLC) form of ownership. His motivation was asset protection. He wanted to take steps to protect, as much as possible, each real estate asset from liabilities from creditors and lawsuits. He structured it so that each property was owned by its own separate LLC entity. For tax purposes, these assets were treated as partnerships (if they involved other owners) or as "disregarded entities" (if he was the sole owner). His spouse owns some of these LLC interests.

Now they are interested in creating a strategy that will allow them to ultimately pass assets to their adult children while minimizing gift and estate taxes. They are in a position in which they can take advantage of the strategies outlined above to

continues ▶

achieve these objectives. They can transfer minority interests in one or more of the LLCs to grantor-retained annuity trusts (GRATs). These will receive valuation discounts because they are minority interests as well as for lack of marketability because they are ownership interest in a closely held entity.

He transfers to a 10-year GRAT a 20 percent interest in an LLC that owns a NYC investment real estate property worth $5 million and retains an annuity interest in the GRAT of $50,000 per year for the 10-year period. The value of the gift is only $382,000. The property is generating a free cash flow of 5 percent and has an assumed annual growth rate of 3 percent. Therefore, it is anticipated that the remainder passing for the benefit of the children at the end of 10 years would be $1,265,300. Even though the value of the property may grow by only about a quarter over 10 years, the value passing to the benefit of the children at the end of 10 years would be more than three times the gift tax value.

At the same time, our client's 62-year-old spouse transferred a 20 percent interest in this same LLC to a GRAT for 15 years, in which she retained the right to receive an annual annuity payment of $64,000 per year. The present value of her gift was less than $58,000, but the value of her interest passing for the children's benefit in 15 years will likely exceed $1 million—a multiple of more than 17 times the value of the gift for gift tax purposes.

As a result of these two transfers (while they are in their 60s and 70s), these clients will be transferring to their children property that will ultimately be worth approximately $2.25 million—but with a total taxable gift value of only $440,000. During the interim term period of the GRATs, they will have retained annual income for themselves of $114,000 per year for the first 10 years and $64,000 per year for the following five years. This tied in with their income objectives established during the planning stage.

One of the requirements for the successful gift and estate tax savings associated with GRATs is that the grantors survive the term period. If not, then the value of the GRAT assets at the time of death will be included in their taxable estate, and it will be as if no transfer took place at all. This means that the term of the GRAT should be well within the anticipated life expectancy based on the grantors' health at the time the GRAT is established. Also, by purchasing term life insurance for each of the clients, we created a hedge against premature death. The term insurance was purchased by an irrevocable life insurance trust (ILIT) and is not part of the clients' taxable estate.

A personal residence GRIT, in the form of a qualified personal residence trust (QPRT), may be very useful in transferring future appreciation potential to G2 and G3, especially in times when values have been depressed.

Qualified Personal Residence Trust (QPRT)
Value of residence: $1,000,000
Age of grantor at beginning of trust: 65
Term of trust: 10 years
Federal discount rate: 3.4 percent (July 2009)
Present value of the remainder interest calculated under the regulations: $562,040
Value of the taxable gift: $562,040
Illustrated value in 10 years, passing to G2 or G3: $1,480,244
Future value removed from estate in 10 years: $918,204
Potential gift and estate tax savings: $459,102

The trust income, if any, will be taxable to the grantor but also allows for the deduction of mortgage interest and property tax payments made by the trustee during the retained interest period.

Charitable Lead Annuity Trust (CLAT)
Split-Interest Gifts
The ownership interest in an asset can be split or divided into two parts, a stream of income payable for one or more lifetimes or a term of years (the income interest) and the principal remaining after the income term (the remainder interest). In a split-interest gift, one portion is given in the charity, and the other portion is retained.

Charitable Remainder Plans
The charitable lead trust (CLAT) is the charitable equivalent of the GRAT, outlined and illustrated above. However, the key difference is that the grantor does not retain the annuity interest for his or her personal use but rather gives it for the use of a tax-qualified charity. A donor may transfer assets to an irrevocable charitable lead annuity (CLAT). The trust then pays a fixed dollar amount to a qualified charity for either a set number of years or the lifetimes of individuals. When the trust has ended, the remaining assets are distributed to the donor, his or her spouse or heirs, or others.

The trust must pay out the same dollar amount each year, without regard to its earnings. If the trust earns more than it pays out to the charitable beneficiary, those extra earnings (and asset appreciation) will pass to the noncharitable beneficiaries (G2, for example) without additional estate or gift taxes.

Valuation of assets is required only at the time the assets are transferred to the CLAT. Ideally, assets in the CLAT should have both income potential (to make the required payments to the charitable beneficiary) and growth potential (to pass long-term appreciation to the ultimate beneficiaries with a minimum of estate or gift taxes).

After the lead (income) period has expired, if the beneficiary of the trust is someone other than the donor or his or her spouse, there may be a taxable gift. The gift tax would be based on the present value of the beneficiaries' right to receive the trust remainder at some future time. This calculation is dependent upon the term of the trust, the amount payable each year to the charity, and the AFR (applicable federal rate) at the time of the transfer.

Example:

> Wealth transfer using CLAT with and without discount for minority-interest ownership and lack of marketability (assumed 20 percent):

Assumptions
Undiscounted value of assets: $1,000,000
Where valuation discount applies: $800,000
Annual gift to charity by CLAT: $50,000
Age of grantor: G1 can be any age in this example
Federal discount rate (AFR): 3.4 percent
Overall annual income and growth rate over term: 8 percent

	CLAT Term	Discount (%)	Current Valuation	Value for Gift Tax Purposes	Illustrated Value to Family at End of Term
1	10 years	0	$1,000,000	$582,065	$1,434,596
2	15 years	0	$1,000,000	$420,010	$1,814,563
3	20 years	0	$1,000,000	$282,905	$2,372,358
4	10 years	20	$800,000	$382,065	$1,434,596
5	15 years	20	$800,000	$220,010	$1,814,563
6	20 years	20	$800,000	$82,905	$2,372,858

As the chart above demonstrates, the longer the charitable lead (income) term is, the lower the current value for gift tax purposes will be. Done correctly, the future value at the end of the term will pass to the family free of gift and estate taxes.

One advantage of the CLT over the GRAT is estate tax treatment if the grantor dies during the charitable lead period. The GRAT assets will largely or entirely be included in the grantor's taxable estate if he or she does not survive the term period. However, this is generally not the case if the grantor dies during the charitable term period. This is a significant advantage for the CLT.

Also note that for both the GRAT and the CLT, the basis in the hands of the trust, as well as that in the family after the term is over, is G1's tax basis at the time of transfer. However, it is possible in both types of trusts to structure them so that G1 will be required to pay all income and capital gain taxes during the term period. These tax payments on behalf of the trust further enhance the value of the trust but are not considered taxable transfers to the trust or its remainder beneficiaries (G2) under current tax rules.

A donor establishing a CLT must consider these issues:

- **Income tax deduction:** If certain requirements are met, an income tax deduction is allowed for the value of the income passing to charity. With a grantor trust, the donor is considered the owner of the trust (taxable on the income under the grantor trust rules) and is allowed the tax deduction, subject to certain percentage of AGI limitations. If the trust is a nongrantor trust, the trust itself is permitted an unlimited tax deduction for distributions to qualified charities. If these requirements are not met, no charitable income tax deduction is allowed to either the donor or the trust.
- **Remainder interest:** At the end of the trust term, should the assets remaining in the trust revert to the donor or pass to other individuals, such as the donor's heirs?
- **Generation-skipping transfer tax (GSTT):** A taxable event for GSTT purposes will occur if the individuals who ultimately receive the assets when the trust terminates are considered to be "skip" persons, such as the donor's grandchildren or a later generation.

Estate Tax Reduction

Charitable lead trusts typically provide a means of transferring assets to G1 or even G2, with substantial valuation discounts. The valuation and transfer tax benefits associated with the example above are generally available for transfers to

CLTs during lifetime (inter vivos) as well as at death through a will or other type of testamentary substitute, such as a trust that creates the CLAT at the time of death.

For individuals who are already committed to making regular charitable gifts and/or who plan to do so at death, the charitable lead trust is an amazing tax bonus allowing them to also make discounted, deferred transfers to heirs. This is a particularly valuable tool when initiated during a low-interest-rate environment.

Charitable lead unitrust (CLUT): G1 transfers assets to an irrevocable charitable lead unitrust (CLUT), which then pays a fixed percentage of its assets to a qualified charity for either a set number of years or the lifetimes of individuals. When the term of the trust has ended, the remaining assets are distributed to the donor, his or her spouse or heirs, or other individuals.

Unlike the CLAT, valuation of the CLUT assets is required every year to determine the amount of the payment for the year. Payments to charity will vary from year to year, depending upon the investment performance and expenses of the trust. The CLUT still provides many of the potential income and estate tax benefits associated with the CLAT.

Charitable trusts with retained income interest for G1 and family:

When G1 retains the right to the income but transfers his or her rights in the remainder to a trust, it is called a charitable remainder trust.

To qualify for an income tax deduction, the trust must be a unitrust, an annuity trust, a pooled income fund, or a charitable gift annuity.

- **Charitable remainder unitrust:** In this type of trust, the donor retains a right to a fixed *percentage* of the fair-market value of the trust assets, with the trust assets being revalued annually. If the value of the assets increases, so does the annual payout and vice versa.
- **Charitable remainder annuity trust:** This trust is similar to the unitrust but instead pays a fixed *dollar* amount each year.
- **Pooled income fund:** Assets are transferred to a common investment fund maintained by the charity. Each donor receives annually a share of the income from the fund, in proportion to the contribution made. These annual payments continue for the lifetimes of the donor and spouse. At death, the corpus of the donor's gift, together with any capital gains, passes to the charity. Payments will increase or decrease with the investment performance of the fund.

- **Charitable gift annuity:** The donor transfers the asset directly to the charity, in exchange for the charity's agreement to a pay fixed lifetime annuity.

The amount of the income tax deduction is dependent upon the percentage of the income interest and the period over which it will be paid (usually the life of the donor and his or her spouse). This is determined from the mortality tables published by the government.

Income Tax Savings

The gift of an asset to a charity generally results in federal income tax deduction, which should decrease the tax due and increase the amount of the net after-tax income for the year. However, charitable contributions are not always 100 percent deductible against an individual's federal income tax liability.

Limits on Annual Charitable Deduction

Federal law limits the amount that is deductible for the year in which the gift is made, based upon one's adjusted gross income (AGI). If the limit is exceeded for the year, any excess deduction can generally be carried forward for up to five years.

If combined charitable contributions for the year do not exceed 20 percent of AGI, they may all be deducted. If, however, contributions exceed 20 percent of AGI, the deduction may be limited to 50, 30, or 20 percent of AGI, depending upon the type of property given and the type of charitable organization receiving the gift. In no event can the deduction exceed 50 percent of the donor's AGI for the year.

Limits on Itemized Deductions

As AGI increases, federal law also acts to reduce certain itemized deductions, including charitable contributions.

Under EGTRRA of 2001, however, this reduction in deductibility is gradually phased out by one-third in 2006–2007 and by two-thirds in 2008–2009. In 2010, there is no reduction to any itemized deduction, regardless of the level of income. However, unless the law is changed, the prior rules will again apply in 2011.

Income Tax Deduction for Split-Interest Gifts

Determining the federal income tax deduction for a "split-interest" gift (i.e., a charitable remainder or charitable lead trust) can be complicated. The key factors involved are:

- How long the charity must wait before it benefits

- How much income is paid to the beneficiaries each year
- The prevailing interest rates at the time of the gift (as indicated by the applicable federal rate)

Charitable Gifts and Estate Taxation Techniques

Gifts to a charity or to a charitable remainder trust can reduce one's taxable estate by not only the value of the gift but also its potential appreciation.

If the donor retains the right to the income, as in a charitable remainder trust, the estate tax savings will not be as large. However, the donor (or donors) may choose to make gifts of the income each year to children or grandchildren or to a trust on their behalf.

If certain requirements are met, these gifts will qualify for the annual gift tax exclusion of $13,000 from each donor to as many qualified beneficiaries as there are under the terms of the trust.

The chart below illustrates the potential savings, based on a hypothetical situation.
Assumptions:
Current estate size: $5,000,000
Estate growth rate: 6 percent
Value of charitable gift: $500,000
Year of death: 2009
Applicable credit: $1,455,800

Years from Now	Taxable Estate Without the Gift	Taxable Estate With the Gift	Federal Estate Tax Without the Gift	Federal Estate Tax With the Gift	Savings in Federal Estate Taxes with Gift
Now	$5,000,000	$4,500,000	$675,000	$450,000	$225,000
5	$6,691,128	$6,022,015	$1,436,008	$1,134,907	$301,101
10	$8,954,238	$8,058,815	$2,454,407	$2,051,467	$402,941
15	$11,982,791	$10,784,512	$3,817,256	$3,278,030	$539,226
20	$16,035,677	$14,432,110	$5,641,055	$4,919,449	$721,605
25	$21,459,354	$19,313,418	$8,081,709	$7,116,038	$965,671
30	$28,717,456	$25,845,710	$11,347,855	$10,055,570	$1,292,286
35	$38,430,434	$34,587,391	$15,718,695	$13,989,326	$1,729,370

Tax-savings techniques associated with charitable remainder trusts at the time of sale of real estate investment property, as well as for transfer from G1 to G2 and G3

A taxpayer (G1) can contribute a highly appreciated asset such as investment real estate to a charitable remainder trust and receive a current income tax deduction.

The trustee can sell the appreciated asset without paying any capital gain tax and can then reinvest the entire proceeds in order to produce income for the trust's income beneficiaries, such as G1 and their children (G2), depending on ages.

This strategy is not an all-or-nothing choice. For example, G1 might transfer only a partial interest in a building, LLC, or partnership to a charitable remainder trust, or they might transfer a portion to a charitable remainder *annuity* trust (CRAT), which would provide a lifetime income benefit only to G1, and also transfer a portion to a charitable remainder *unitrust* (CRUT), with an income benefit to G1 for life, followed by an income interest to G2 for life. At the same time, G1 might retain a portion of the property in their name. The CRAT- and CRUT-owned portions would be sold with no current tax recognition at sale, whereas the portion retained in their name would be taxable as proceeds are received. This type of planning might also result in some valuation discounts on the third piece if it was being transferred to a grantor-retained annuity trust (GRAT), as outlined above. In fact, that third piece could also be transferred to a charitable *lead* annuity trust (CLAT), with all the attendant gift tax advantages outlined above.

The trust's payout will typically be higher than it would be if G1 had sold the asset outright and paid all the associated taxes on the gain. This, coupled with the income tax deduction, can create a substantial increase in cash flow after the sale.

Some taxpayers use a portion of the increased cash flow to purchase a life insurance policy (outside of the estate) to replace all or part of the value of the asset transferred to the trust.

Party	Benefit
G1 (and spouse)	Increased cash flow during retirement years
G2/G3	Same size or larger inheritance (with insurance)
Favorite charity	Receives remaining assets after income term ends
Internal Revenue Service	Receives less income and estate tax

Charitable Remainder Unitrust (CRUT)

A charitable remainder unitrust (CRUT) is an irrevocable trust that pays a fixed percentage of the value of its holdings each year to a beneficiary such as the donor of the trust assets, his or her spouse, child, etc. Unlike the fixed-dollar payment of a charitable remainder annuity trust, the unitrust payments will fluctuate with the changing asset balance in the trust, reflecting year-to-year investment performance.

After the death of the income beneficiaries or at the end of a set number of years (no more than 20), whatever assets remain in the trust are distributed to the charities named in the trust. Additional contributions can be made to the trust in later years if desired.

CRUT Variations

The standard form of CRUT requires payment of the full stated percentage throughout the life of the trust, even if assets must be liquidated. Other CRUT variations include:

- **Net-income CRUT:** A CRUT may be drafted to pay out less than the established percentage if the trust income during the year is less than the required payout percentage. This shortage can be made up in later years when the trust earns more than the required payout percentage.
- **"Flip" CRUT:** Under IRS regulations, a CRUT may begin life as a net-income trust and, at some predetermined future date or triggering event, permanently convert ("flip") to a standard unitrust. A "flip" CRUT is an option for an individual seeking a current income tax deduction, tax-deferred buildup, and increased income at a later date.

Charitable Remainder Annuity Trust (CRAT)

A charitable remainder annuity trust (CRAT) is an irrevocable trust that pays a fixed dollar amount each year to a beneficiary, such as the donor of the trust assets or his or her spouse, child, etc. This fixed dollar amount is determined by applying the trust's stated percentage payout, e.g., 5 percent, 6 percent, etc., to the value of the asset initially transferred by the donor.

After the death of the income beneficiaries or at the end of a set number of years, whatever assets that remain in the trust are distributed to the charity's name in the trust. If additional contributions are desired in later years, new trusts must be established.

Income Tax Considerations
The charitable income tax deduction is based on the current value of the charity's right to receive the trust assets at some time in the future (a remainder interest). There are several factors in determining this value.

- The first factor is the estimated length of time the charity must wait, for example, a term of years (10, 15, 20, etc.) or for the donor's or other person's lifetime.
- Another factor is the percentage rate payable to the income beneficiaries each year and how frequently it is paid, e.g., annually, monthly, etc. Obviously, the higher the rate of payout is, the less there will be for the charity and, therefore, the smaller the charitable deduction will be.
- The current rate of return on investments as determined by the applicable federal (midterm) rates (AFR) is also an important factor.

All of these factors are applied to government tables to determine the current value of the charitable deduction. If the charitable deduction exceeds a certain percentage of the donor's adjusted gross income for the year of the gift, that portion must be carried over into future years.

Gift Tax Considerations
If the income from the CRAT is payable to someone other than the donor, it may be subject to federal gift taxation. If certain requirements are met, the income gift can be made to qualify for the annual tax exclusion of $13,000 per beneficiary. Also, the marital deduction will usually eliminate any gift tax on payments to the donor's spouse.

Estate Tax Considerations
The value of the interest passing to the charity is deductible from the gross estate. If there are income beneficiaries other than the donor and his or her spouse, there may be an estate tax on the value of this income interest.

Installment Sale: Capital Gain Tax at Sale of Real Estate

The installment sale method allows a taxpayer to spread the profit on a sale over the entire period during which the payments are received. Each payment received is treated partly as a return of investment and partly as profit and interest. This relieves the seller of paying tax on income not yet received. The seller must use the installment method or elect not to use it and include all of the gain in the current year.

Imputed Interest

If no interest is charged under the terms of the agreement, the IRS imputes interest to the transaction. This means that even if the seller does not collect any interest on the transaction, the IRS will pretend that the seller does and require inclusion of the imputed interest in his or her annual income.

Depreciable Property

If the property sold has been subject to excess depreciation (i.e., greater than straight-line depreciation), any recapture of the excess depreciation must be reported in the year of the sale. Any gain in excess of the recaptured amount may be eligible for installment treatment. When the parties are related, installment sale treatment is available for sales of depreciated property only if it can be demonstrated that tax avoidance was not a principal purpose for the installment sale.

Sales to Related Parties

Any installment sale to a related party who then sells (or otherwise disposes of) the property may cancel the installment reporting of the first sale unless at least two years have passed since the first sale and the property is not marketable securities. See IRC Sec. 453(e).

Sales by Dealers

Sales of real or personal property by a dealer or anyone who regularly sells property on the installment plan cannot be reported on the installment method.

Advantage of Installment Sales

- By spreading income over two or more tax years, it may allow the gain to be taxed in lower tax brackets.

- Even if no taxes are saved, if the payment can be postponed for one or more years, the deferred tax dollars can earn income until they become due.
- Potential future appreciation of the assets may be removed from the seller's estate.
- One may be able to shift high-income-producing assets to a family member in a lower tax bracket.

Private Annuity

A private annuity is a contract between two individuals to exchange a valuable asset for a lifetime income.

A Typical Example

G1 (annuitant) transfers a direct interest or interest in an entity with investment real estate (usually highly appreciated) to G2 or G3 (payor). G1 (payee) receives in return an unsecured promise to pay an annual sum for the lifetime of G1.

- If the annuity payment is large enough, there will be no gift tax.
- The annuity factor is dependent upon G1's age.
- G1 can make annual gifts to a child to assist in meeting the annual payments.
- Payments to G1 are partially income tax free, with the remainder taxed as ordinary income, but they are not deductible to the payer.

Estate-Planning Considerations
Advantage

- The asset and future appreciating may be removed from G1's estate without gift tax or estate tax liability.
- G1 gets a lifetime income.
- Some of the payments will be considered a return of capital and not taxable.

Disadvantages

- G1 may live too long, with the payer paying too much for the asset, thus increasing the size of G1's estate.
- Payments are not tax deductible.

- If G2 dies, it may be difficult to collect the payments. A life insurance policy on G2 could guarantee funds.

Joint Purchase of Assets

The technique of a joint purchase of certain assets by a parent and child can bring some very attractive tax results; however, in most cases, it has been eliminated as a family wealth-transfer technique. Here's how it could work:

- A parent and a child find a qualified property. Joint purchases by family members must be limited to a personal residence or tangible property, such as artwork.
- The parent purchases the life income interest, and the child purchases the remainder interest. An IRS Table S gives the allocation percentages based on a rate that varies from month to month, as provided under IRC Sec. 7520.

Assume G1 aged 55 wants to purchase a personal residence with G2 under this type of arrangement. G1 might need to invest 77 percent and G2 only 23 percent. At G1's demise, his or her life income expires, and the asset is not included in the estate—the entire 77 percent paid into the property, plus any appreciation, would be excluded.

Potential Problems
- The return on G2's investment may not be very high if G1 lives beyond life expectancy.

If G1 gives the money to G2 to make the initial purchase, there will be estate and gift tax problems. The IRS will likely treat the transaction as a purchase by G1, with a gift of future interest (the remainder) to G2. Future interest does not qualify for the annual gift tax exclusion. Furthermore, because G2 retained a life income, the IRS may attempt to include the asset in his or her estate.

Life Insurance

As one of my long-term real estate clients aptly told his spouse, "After dealing with estate planning for our family's investment property interest for several generations,

I have learned that these estate-planning strategies work well to help reduce taxes, but they always work better when life insurance is somewhere in the mix."

This was a client who, at age 65, had seen the benefits of good tax planning coupled with life insurance as assets moved down from his parents' estate to him and were now moving down from him to benefit his children and grandchildren. Over the years, he had taken advantage of virtually all of the strategies outlined above, as well some that were no longer available because of changes in tax laws and regulations.

The client did find that the use of life insurance, owned by various trusts outside the insured's taxable estate, added income tax–free dollars to the family's assets that were used to meet estate and income tax bills, to equalize interests for different members of younger generations, and to provide a known stable value that allowed the family to plan with greater certainty.

The financial strategies available to you as a real estate investor are both many and varied. To maximize these tools, you'll want to develop a personalized plan and do a thorough evaluation of your own financial situation *before* jumping into the game. Do your homework and find a reputable, experienced financial professional to work with and you'll soon be benefiting from the personal wealth advantages associated with real estate investment.

Appendix A
Resources for NYC Real Estate Investors

Online resources for investors can be found throughout this book, but here are more resources to help you navigate the landscape:

ASSOCIATIONS
National Association of Realtors
http://www.realtor.org

National Association of Housing Cooperatives
http://www.coophousing.org

ECONOMIC INFORMATION
UCLA Anderson Forecast
http://uclaforecast.com

U.S. Census Bureau Census of Housing
http://www.census.gov/hhes/www/housing/census/histcensushsg.html

FEDERAL STATISTICS AND INFORMATION
U.S. Department of Housing and Urban Development (HUD)
http://www.hud.gov

U.S. Bureau of Labor Statistics (BLS)
http://www.bls.gov

U.S. Census Bureau
http://www.census.gov

Finance and Tax Planning
The Financial Planning Association
http://www.fpanet.org

National Association of Personal Financial Advisors
http://www.napfa.org

U.S. Securities and Exchange Commission EDGAR Database
http://www.sec.gov/edgar.shtml

Federation of Exchange Accommodators: 1031 Like-Kind Exchanges
http://www.1031.org

Foreclosure Information
RealtyTrac.com
http://www.realtytrac.com

Foreclosure.com
http://www.foreclosure.com

Mortgage and Market Trends
HSH Associates, Financial Publishers
http://www.hsh.com

Real Trends
http://www.realtrends.com

New York Housing Sites

A Landlord's Guide to the NYC Housing Court
http://www.nycourts.gov/courts/nyc/housing/pdfs/Landlordbooklet.pdf

Department of Buildings BIS Site
BIS is the Buildings Information System, the Department of Buildings' database of licensee information, complaints, Department of Buildings and Environmental Control Board (ECB) violations, boilers, and property profile and construction application information.
http://www.nyc.gov/html/dob/html/bis/bis.shtml

New York State Division of Housing and Community Renewal (DHCR)
The Division of Housing and Community Renewal is responsible for the supervision, maintenance, and development of affordable low- and moderate-income housing in New York State.
http://www.dhcr.state.ny.us

Automated City Register Information System (ACRIS)
The Department of Finance collects property taxes and other property-related charges, maintains title records and tax maps, conducts lien sales, and collects real property transfer and mortgage-recording taxes. Finance also values all New York City residential and commercial properties and information on condo/co-op comparable rental income. Tax rates are set each year by the city council and applied to property values to determine each owner's annual tax liability.
http://www.nyc.gov/html/dof/html/jump/acris.shtml

New York City Rent Guidelines Board (RGB)
From this site, you can download research reports, view the rent guidelines, send your housing questions to staff by e-mail, view an RGB meeting schedule and organizational chart, or read publications such as the Attorney General's Landlord/Tenant Guide, DHCR's Fact Sheets for Stabilized Housing, or the Housing Maintenance Code.
http://www.housingnyc.com

New York State Unified Court System
The online database for "housing court" provides information on tenant actions, complaints, and other issues related to specific properties in the city. The court's housing division handles only residential landlord and tenant cases, while commercial landlord and tenant cases and ejectment actions are handled on the civil side.
http://www.courts.state.ny.us/courts/nyc/civil/index.shtml

NY State Division of Housing and Community Renewal Forms
http://www.dhcr.state.ny.us/Forms/Rent

NYC Department of Housing Preservation and Development (HPD)
http://www.nyc.gov/html/hpd

New York City Housing Authority (NYCHA)
http://www.nyc.gov/nycha

New York City Department of City Planning
http://www.nyc.gov/html/dcp/home.html

New York City Department of Buildings
http://www.nyc.gov/buildings

NYC Rent-Stabilization/Control
http://www.dhcr.state.ny.us/Rent

Appendix B
Real Estate Glossary

Abatement: A reduction or decrease in the value of a property that affects its market value or the amount of rent that may be charged to a tenant.

Absorption rate: The number of properties within a property development (e.g., a tract of land on which houses are being built; a building in which apartments are being converted to condominiums) that can be sold in a particular market within a certain time.

Abut: To share a common (property) boundary or even share a portion of that boundary.

Acceptance: A positive (and voluntary) response to an offer or counteroffer for a property that sets out price and terms.

Access: The right to enter a property. This may be restricted to certain times and to certain categories of people (e.g., those who read gas or electric meters or deliver the mail).

Actual age: The years a building has been in existence (i.e., its chronological age). Its effective age is a more subjective judgment; it reflects the condition of the building (i.e., how well it has been maintained).

After-tax cash flow: The net profit of an income property after direct costs (e.g., interest on the mortgage, taxes, maintenance) have been subtracted.

Agent: Anyone who is authorized by a buyer or seller of property to act on that person's behalf in any dealings with third parties. The third party may rely on the agreement and assurances of the agent as being binding on the person represented.

Appraisal: An estimate of the value of a property on a certain date, usually provided by a qualified appraiser, after both an inspection of the property and a comparison of that property with other comparable properties that have recently been sold.

Appreciation: The increase in value of a property over time. This increase can be the result of many factors, such as inflation, additional demand for property resulting from low interest rates, the condition of the market, or the gentrification of a particular area.

Assessed value: The value placed on a property by a tax assessor for the purpose of determining property taxes.

Base rent: The set rent that is paid by a tenant and to which can be added additional fees as set out in the lease (for upkeep, utilities, etc.).

Boundary: The legally determined edge or limit of a property.

Broker: Refers to two kinds of agents: a mortgage broker, who brings potential borrowers together with potential lenders, and a real estate broker, who brings buyers together with sellers. Real estate broker is a professional designation; it requires training and licensing.

Building permit: A permit that is issued by a local government to allow a builder to construct a building or to make improvements to existing structures.

Building restriction: Rules in the building code (zoning restrictions, for example) that control the size, placement, design, and materials of new construction.

Capital gain: An increase in the value of capital property (i.e., property other than a principal residence) on which tax is payable, usually upon sale of the property.

Capital loss: A decrease in the value of capital property (i.e., property other than a principal residence), which the owner may use against capital gains or against regular income when paying his or her taxes, depending on the tax rules.

Cash flow: Net earned income from an income property after all the expenses of holding and carrying the property are paid or factored in.

Certified Property Manager (CPM): Someone who has met the requirements of the Institute of Real Estate Management to manage property. The institute is an affiliate of the National Association of Realtors.

Commitment/commitment letter: A written promise, by a lender or insurance company, to make a loan or insure a loan for a specified amount and on specified terms.

Common-area assessments: A periodic charge (usually monthly) that is levied against owners in a condominium complex. These fees are used by the condominium owners' association to pay for the maintenance of common areas in the building.

Conversion: The changing of an apartment to a condominium unit or the improper taking of another person's property for one's own use (such as moving into a person's vacation home and living there while the person is away).

Co-op: Abbreviated term for "cooperative," a form of ownership in which the occupants of individual units in a building have shares in the cooperative corporation that owns the entire property. Co-ops are still popular in large American cities, such as New York and Chicago, but condominiums are the more usual form of "apartment" ownership in most American cities and suburbs.

Debt-equity ratio: A comparison of what is owed on a property with its equity (i.e., the current market value of the property less the amount owed on the mortgage or loan).

Debt financing: The purchase of a property using any kind of credit rather than paying cash.

Depreciation: The decrease in value of a property over time, which can also lead to a reduction in the owner's taxes (i.e., a capital loss).

Deterioration: The effects of time and wear and tear on a property or neglect of that property, causing its value to decrease unless some action is taken to counteract and correct these effects.

Encumbrance: Any right, lien, or charge attached to and binding on a property. An encumbrance can affect the owner's ability or right to sell that property until such time as it is removed.

Equity: The market value of a property, less the debts of that property. Possible debts include the principal and accumulated interest on the mortgage, unpaid taxes, and a home equity loan.

Fair-market value: The price that is likely to be agreed on by a buyer and a seller for a specific property at a specific time. This price is typically arrived at by considering the sales prices of comparable properties in the area, taking into consideration any special features of or upgrades to the property in question.

Fixed expenses: These are the certain costs of owning and operating a property. The cost of painting a house is not a fixed expense, but the property tax on that house is.

Flipping: The practice whereby a property is purchased in the hope that it can be sold quickly for a higher price.

Foreclosure: A proceeding that is usually instigated by a lender, in a court or not, to cancel all rights and title of an owner in a particular property when that owner has defaulted on payment of a mortgage.

Income property: Any property that is developed (or purchased) specifically to produce

income for its owner, such as an apartment building.

Judgment: A decision rendered by a court. If a monetary settlement is involved, it may become a lien on the property of the losing party.

Legal description: A description of property that is acceptable in a court of law.

Legal title: The rights of ownership that are conferred on a person when he or she purchases a piece of property. These rights may be defended against any other competing interests.

Lessee: The tenant under a lease; someone who leases property.

Lessor: The owner of the property.

Loan-to-value ratio: The difference between the appraised value of a property and the amount being loaned on a mortgage.

Maintenance costs: The expense required to keep a property in a good state of repair.

Market price: The amount actually paid for a property.

Market rent: The amount that an owner can reasonably charge someone who wishes to lease a property.

Net operating income (NOI): The income from a property that is left after the costs of **maintaining and servicing that property are subtracted.**

Normal wear and tear: Damage to a property that is the result of neither carelessness nor maliciousness but simply reasonable use and the passage of time.

Occupancy: The physical possession of a building or property.

On-site improvements: Any work performed on a property that adds to its utility, value, or attractiveness.

Permit: A government body's written permission allowing changes to a particular property when such changes are regulated by that government body.

Redevelop: To remove existing improvements (usually buildings) on a piece of land and replace them with new, more useful or more profitable improvements.

Rehabilitate: To restore or refurbish real estate.

Rent: The payments that are made by a tenant to a landlord for the right to occupy premises owned by the landlord, or the act of leasing premises from a landlord.

Rent control: Refers to laws or ordinances that set price controls on the renting of residential housing. The rent control program generally applies to residential buildings constructed before February 1947 in municipalities that have not declared an end to the postwar rental housing emergency.

Rent stabilization: A type of rent control that in New York City applies to apartments in buildings of six or more units and built between February 1, 1947, and January 1, 1974.

Reserve fund: The fund that is maintained by a condominium corporation (or a cooperative) for future contingencies, such as unforeseen major structural repairs to the condominium building, which are very expensive.

Rezoning: The reclassification of a property or a particular district from one kind of use to another. An area might be rezoned from commercial to residential, which would allow former office buildings to be converted into residential condominiums.

Sale price: The amount of money that is paid by the buyer to the seller for a particular property.

Sever/severance: To divide one property from another so that each may be sold or used separately.

Sublease: A rental contract between a tenant and someone who rents from that tenant.

Tax: A government levy against real property. If taxes are unpaid, the government may attach a lien to the property. Such liens are regarded as preeminent (they are given priority over mortgages).

Tax base: The assessed valuation of a piece of real property. This value is multiplied by the government's tax rate to determine the amount of property tax due.

Tenancy at will: A kind of tenancy, created by written agreement, that allows the landlord to evict the tenant at any time. This kind of tenancy might come into effect for a condemned building for which the date of demolition has not been established by the owner or local government authority.

Triple-net lease: A rental agreement that requires the tenant to pay all the operating costs of the premises.

Unit: A single dwelling in a larger complex. The term is most often used with regard to a condominium project. It refers to a unit (or, in a rental building, an apartment) that is reserved for the exclusive use of the owner.

Up-rent potential: An estimate of how much the rent on a particular property is likely to be raised over a given period. Such an estimate might be offered to a potential tenant as an inducement to sign a lease.

Vacancy rate: A calculation, expressed as a percentage, of all the available rental units in a particular area and at a certain time that are not rented.

Variable expenses: The operating costs of a property that are not fixed, such as heating costs, which can change dramatically depending on whether a winter is mild or severe.

Zone: An area of a city (or county) that is set aside for a certain purpose, such as an industrial zone.

References Cited

Alston, R. M., J. R. Kearl, and M. B. Vaughan. 1992. Is there a consensus among economists in the 1990s? *American Economic Review* 82:203–209.

Bresiger, G. 2006. Housing socialism. Pts. 1, 2. Future of Freedom Foundation: Fairfax, VA. http://www.fff.org/freedom/fd0606d.asp, http://www.fff.org/freedom/fd0607d.asp.

Cravatts, R. L. 2003. Rent control doesn't work. *International Real Estate Digest.* http://www.ired.com/news/2003/rentcontrol.htm.

Ferguson, S. 2005. Turning tenements into mansions: landlords try to mass-evict tenants. *The Villager* 75, July 13–20. http://www.thevillager.com/villager_115/turningtenementsinto.html.

Gerber, M. 1995. *The e-myth revisited: why most small businesses don't work and what to do about it.* New York: HarperCollins.

Lindbeck, A. 1972. *The political economy of the new left.* New York: Harper & Row.

Mildner, G., and P. D. Salins. 1991. Does rent control help the poor? *City Journal*, Winter. http://www.city-journal.org/article01.php?aid=1616.

Murray, B. 2009. With demand growing nationwide, NY state first to receive stimulus funding for affordable housing. *Commercial Property Executive*, April 8. http://www.cpexecutive.com/cpn/content_display/business-specialties/development/e3ib022d07c4ee57d29e29bb656f137a375.

National Multi Housing Council (NMHC). 2009. Rent control. http://www.nmhc.org/Content/ContentList.cfm?NavID=395.

New York City Department of City Planning (DCP). 2010. Hudson Yards. http://www.nyc.gov/html/dcp/html/hyards/hymain.shtml.

Pollakowski, H. O. 2003. Rent control and housing investment: evidence from deregulation in Cambridge, Massachusetts. *Civic Report*, no. 36. http://www.manhattan-institute.org/pdf/cr_36.pdf.

Salins, P. D. 1996. New York City's housing gap. *Civic Report*, no. 2. http://www.manhattan-institute.org/html/cr_2.htm.

Scanlon, R., and H. Cohen. 2008. Cutting the high cost of housing. *Gotham Gazette*, September. http://www.gothamgazette.com/article/housing/20080916/10/2647.

About the Authors

Peter Von Der Ahe

began his career at the Real Estate Consulting Group of Arthur Andersen in New York. His work with this group, which focused on property valuation, financing, and loan underwriting, provided him with experience working on office, retail, and apartment transactions worth a combined value of over $700 million.

As Vice President of Investments at Marcus & Millichap Real Estate Investment Services in New York City, Von Der Ahe and his team of affiliated brokers understand that clients operating in the New York City marketplace need the most sophisticated and informed agents available to successfully execute their investment goals.

With a commitment to integrity, Von Der Ahe operates with his ears to the ground and delivers first hand information on the nuances of the market to readers to allow for intelligent and financially rewarding choices.

Von Der Ahe's market commentary can be consistently found in *The New York Times*, *Crain's New York*, *New York Post*, *The Commercial Observer*, *Real Estate Weekly*, *Globe Street*, and many other industry publications.

Von Der Ahe is also a professionally trained jazz and improvisational pianist and has performed in off Broadway productions in both New York and Los Angeles. He currently lives in New York City with his wife and two boys.

Glen Kunofsky

is a senior vice president and senior director of the National Retail Group and Net Leased Properties Group of Marcus & Millichap Real Estate Investment Services. He has a long track record of acquiring, managing and brokering commercial properties throughout the United States and is an authority in the field of Net Leases and Sale-Leaseback Transactions.

With unparalleled experience Kunofsky is recognized as a leader in his industry. Over the past five years he has closed over 1,200 properties with an aggregate value of approximately $1.5 billion. Kunofsky has earned acknowledgments as the #1 Agent Companywide, #1 Producing Retail Property Agent, and Top Investment Professional Nationally at Marcus & Millichap, NY Brokerage All Stars, and Real Estate NY 40 Under 40.

Mark McGorry

JD, CFP, CPC, CLU, AEP entered the financial services field in 1968. He is a financial consultant specializing in estate, tax, pension, insurance, investment, and business planning. He frequently works alongside clients' other advisors (accountants, attorneys, financial planners, including insurance agents and investment advisors) to develop, design, and implement advanced planning strategies in these areas.

McGorry is a frequent lecturer for professional associations. He is a frequently published author, with articles appearing in various professional publications and journals. He was the founding editor, as well as Editor-in-Chief of *Distribution Advisor,* a monthly newsletter published by Aspen Publishers focusing on integrating planning for distributions from IRAs, TSAs, and Qualified Plans with the clients' overall wealth management and financial planning. He has also published articles concerning pension and estate planning for the *CPA Journal* of the New York State Society of Certified Public Accountants. McGorry has also been a columnist and contributing editor for *All Taxes Plus Professional Advisors Update.*

FAMILY SECRETS
SECRET STRATEGIES FOR NEW YORK CITY MULTIFAMILY INVESTING

For More Information
www.famsecretsbook.com

Peter Von Der Ahe
www.famsecretsbook.com

phone: 212.430.5114

email: peter@famsecretsbook.com

Glen Kunofsky
www.nnnpro.com

phone: 212.430.5115

email: glen.kunofsky@NNNPro.com

Mark McGorry
www.wealthpartners.com

phone: (212) 689-6700

email: mmcgorry@wealthpartners.com

I